BREATH OF LIFE

By
COLIN P. SISSON

TOTAL PRESS LTD.

© COPYRIGHT 1989 by Colin P. Sisson

All Rights Reserved

ISBN 0-9597930-0-3

All enquiries about Breath Integration or Rebirthing or for obtaining copies of this book, refer to the rear of this book for a list of Distributors, or write to:

TOTAL PRESS LTD.
P.O.Box 7264
Wellesley Street,
Auckland 1
New Zealand.

ACKNOWLEDGEMENTS

KATHRYN G. RICHARDSON-SISSON
My companion who shared so much of herself and contributed so much towards my healing and self discovery. Thank you Kathryn.

MARGARET MULQUEEN
Who contributed so much of her wisdom and love to the creation of this book. Who shared so much in my growing. Thank you Margaret.

JANE DAVIES
Through her clarity and dedication to truth has made a major contribution to not only this book, but to the Breath Integration Process. Thank you Jane.

LORRAINE ANDERSON
Thank you Lorraine for all the love and support of my work. You have been a great Inspiration.

VICKY WHITE
Thank you Vicky for all the excellent Proof-Reading and grammatical skills.

MICHAEL FREEDMAN
Through his guidance and teachings, I was able to experience the delights of my Inner Self. Thank you Michael.

LEONARD ORR
The Founder of Rebirthing. Thank you once again Leonard, for your inspirations and dedication to the enlightenment of human consciousness.

GEORGE I. GURDJIEFF AND PETER D. OUSPENSKY
Through their writings and teachings, I was greatly inspired to reach and search further than the ordinary phenomena of this created Universe. Thank you!

Thank you all those who have touched my life through my work and my healing. You are too numerous to mention and include all my Family, Friends, clients and associates.

I also thank all those who have purchased my previous books. You have supported, inspired and enabled me to produce more of my work. Thank you.

BREATH OF LIFE

CONTENTS

Page

Acknowledgements
Contents
Foreword

Ch. 1.	I Dream of Greater Things	1
Ch. 2.	Defenses, Our Protective Barriers	9
Ch. 3.	Breath Integration	19
Ch. 4.	Integration and Integrity	27
Ch. 5.	Conscious Connected Breathing	43
Ch. 6.	Higher Consciousness	53
Ch. 7.	Total Acceptance	65
Ch. 8.	The Art of Surrender	75
Ch. 9.	Perfection	81
Ch. 10.	Self Responsibility	95
Ch. 11.	Manipulation as a Defense	107
Ch. 12.	The Manipulating Triangle	121
Ch. 13.	Beliefs	133
Ch. 14.	Personal Laws	143
Ch. 15.	Personal Law Chart	155
Ch. 16.	Commitment	163
Ch. 17.	Sign Posts	173

Appendix 1.	177
Appendix 2.	179
Glossary	181
About the Author	186
List of Book Distributors	188
Bibliography	189

FOREWORD

I wrote this book believing that readers may have already read my previous work, "Rebirthing Made Easy". For those who haven't, refer to the glossary at the rear of this book for definitions of terms.

I dedicate this book to all the wonderful people who have touched my life through my work, my learning, and in my play. You have taken me gently in your arms and carefully nurtured, stretched and loved me until I felt safe enough to express my Perfection to the world.

I bow down to you in gratitude, and trust that I will honour and serve you through these following words.

CHAPTER ONE

I DREAM OF GREATER THINGS

I remember one afternoon in 1980, I was standing on the top of the Waitakere ranges, over-looking Auckland city. My life was a mess. My marriage was breaking up, I was broke, I had few close friends I could share my intimate feelings with, and I was depressed. I had gone for a drive to be on my own, to collect my thoughts and have some space from the difficulties at home.

My car had found it's way into the ranges, and I stopped at a lookout point, where the sprawling city of Auckland looked miniature, and stretched as far as the eye could see.

As I stood there, the city had no impression on me, as I was too wrapped up in how terrible the world and all the people in it were treating me. A classic case of 'poor me syndrome'.

It didn't seem fair, considering all I had done. I had gone to defend my country in Vietnam, only to return to a reception of protestors as if I was a war criminal. I was feeling bitter about that. I loved Rita, but we just couldn't get the marriage working in spite of all the efforts we were both putting into it. And what about all the work I had done in counselling, helping people get their lives together. That was ironic. Here I was telling people how it all was, and I was a mess.

Suddenly, the sun's reflection on a window far below in the city caught my eye. My mind drifted to it. What were the people in that house doing in this precise moment: preparing meals, eating, entertaining friends, watching television, making love, reading? For a few minutes, I forgot about myself and my pain. I had suddenly lifted the horizon of my limited thinking and expanded it to think about what others were doing. I expanded my thoughts even further to consider what half a million Aucklanders could be doing in that instant. And here I was looking down upon them all as if I was some massive giant, or even God. At that point I wasn't Colin Sisson lost in his 'hurt' any more, but someone removed from his pain, yet very present in observing the multiplicity of human life spread below him.

It gave me a sense of vastness I hadn't experienced since I was quite young. This sense of greatness made me realise that the universe is incredibly huge, and that not only am I a part of it, but I am right in the middle of my own personal universe. I got a sense of being present with myself, and was beginning to see I could have some degree of command over my personal world, though I didn't at that point know how to do this.

This experience marked a positive change in my life! I realised for the first time that there was more to life than just what I was feeling, thinking and doing . That I was part of a massive flow of energy which I later defined as 'consciousness'.

What this all taught me was that by simply changing my focus, I could change how I was feeling. Part of my understanding was that somehow feelings were linked to the types of thoughts I focused on. I had read most of the books on positive thinking, and learned that if you think negatively, you get negative results, and the reverse is also true. Yet, one can have

2

all the theory in the world and it means but a drop in the ocean of life. Knowledge on its own means little until one has the actual experience. And here I was on a hill seemingly overlooking the world, with a new sense of myself.

"Oh, if I could dream a dream of great things where I could lift my sight above my squalor and suffering. From henceforth, I will live my life, not as it is, but how it should be." I then changed this to "how it could be." Then I changed it again to "how I want it to be".

"I shall live my life as I want it to be, respecting all others, and creating my own life and my own Reality!"

Join me, dear reader, as we embark on an exciting adventure into the soul, where we can let go of the illusion of suffering and taste the sweetness and Joy of Reality!

One thing I've learnt in my few years on this planet is how people, myself included, spend so much energy and time avoiding certain experiences, and chasing after others. This is not surprising if one is taught that some experiences are good and others are bad. Among the good experiences could be achievement, being loved and approved of, eating, making love, having a profound spiritual experience. Among the bad ones could be being rejected, punished or the threat of punishment, feeling fear, physical pain.

Yet, I am reminded of the words of the Buddha who revealed to the world that an experience is just an experience. It is neither good nor bad, it is neutral; it just is. It is human values and conclusions about each experience which determine whether it is enjoyable or a suffering. The values and judgements we as humans place upon an experience is more important than the experience itself in terms of how it affects us. Think about that for a moment.

It was this very revelation that came to me while standing on a hill over-looking a city all those years ago. I had spent my whole life avoiding pain and chasing happiness, and it hadn't worked. In trying to live my life this way, I had simply suppressed many experiences, along with my life urge, (the will to live). I had attached myself to the illusive concept of finding happiness outside of myself.

It reminds me of the story of a young cat who believed happiness was in its tail. It spend many hours chasing around in circles trying to catch it. One day, an older and wiser cat came along and asked the young cat what he was doing. The young cat replied that happiness was in its tail and once he caught it he would be happy! The older cat said, "I too am wise to the ways of the world and know that happiness is in my tail, but I have observed that the more I chased it, the more it got away from me. So, now I walk content with myself and I notice that it always follows me wherever I go".

Attachment in these terms means a belief that we need something in order to be happy. Attachment to anything in this world whether it be a person, a material possession, or an experience, ultimately leads to suffering, because eventually we grow beyond such things. Life is constantly moving, changing, and to cling to something we believe we need, tends to make it bigger than ourselves in our minds, and its eventual loss makes us feel unhappy, if not devastated.

Some people in order to protect themselves against future

losses, and hurts, wall themselves off from experiences and other people. They build walls, defenses, disassociate and withdraw involvement in life. Being attached is a trap, and yet, we may need to break the container of our ego, and mix with all aspects of life. We may need to become less attached and yet, be more involved with life, and this may be the difference between a free and happy life and one of suffering. Being involved is what life is all about. We get hurt because we form attachments. We walk on freely and happily when we are fully involved but free of attachments. Come into life. Come into experience, the water is fun. Take a risk and try it!

Years ago I was involved with self-improvement seminars. We used to teach that the difference between a successful person and a failure was that the successful person had goals and the failure had none. My thinking has changed considerably since that time. I realise now that failure as a human is impossible. There are many who don't share this understanding and so experience failure in terms of unemployment, lack of money, poor health, alcoholism, drug abuse, unhappy relationships, attempted suicide etc. Their belief in such things keeps them trapped in it. Because they think they have failed in one or two aspects of life, they think they have failed as a human being. They have forgotten about the good things they have experienced in their lives. They have forgotten they are a 'Spiritual Being' and greater than mere temporary aspects of the physical universe.

Here is a definition for failure and success:

Failure is someone else's opinion of how something should not be done!

All success and achievement is self-related and not dependent upon the values of other people or institutions. We can be wise, prosperous and happy simply by thinking that way, and believing in ourselves, based upon our own standards and not someone else's. It is safe to dream of greater things and know you deserve them. If a great Sage-King came to visit your house, how would you treat him? Would you prepare a welcome of decorations, fine food, clean and tidy surroundings? Of course you would, and yet we often deny the great King/Queen-Sage within us. We are so controlled by how other people think. We are so afraid of being rejected by them, ever fearful of their withholding approval, that we give up being in charge of our own lives, and making our own decisions.

So, here is a definition for success:

Success is the ability to experience Love and Joy within ourselves.

The operative word in the last sentence is 'experience'. Often the first step towards experiencing love and joy is to first experience our grief, anger and suffering. In doing this we can eventually release it through the principles in this book and walk away free.

Our ability to experience Love and Joy depends upon how conscious we are and upon how conscious we are willing to be, and how aware we choose to be in the face of every life situation that enters our field of experience. Open up to it for it is there to teach us the 'Glory of the present moment'.

Affirmation:

"I DREAM A DREAM OF GREAT THINGS AND HENCEFORTH, I WILL LIVE MY LIFE AS I WANT TO, RESPECTING ALL OTHERS, AND IN CHARGE OF CREATING MY OWN LIFE AND MY OWN REALITY".

CHAPTER TWO

DEFENSES,
OUR PROTECTIVE BARRIERS

Each individual is made up of a large number of different energies, perceptions, thoughts, emotions, sensations, and matter. These energies exist forming each individual's mind and body as well as defining the boundaries of that person's world with them being at the centre. Each person has many different level s of safety with their already known experience, and this could be called a 'comfort zone', a state in which they feel comfortable with each experience. How well a person knows themselves depends upon how familiar they are with the outer limits of their comfort zones, the boundaries they have already explored and experienced. The person who has never made a mistake, who prefers to stay within the confines of their comfort zone hasn't experienced life, hasn't allowed themselves to touch the individual boundaries, that await their exploration and expression.

Physically, these boundaries are experienced as muscle tension, restricted movement and intense physical sensations. Emotional boundaries are experienced as addictions (cravings), and fear. Intellectual boundaries are experienced as beliefs in limitation (dogma), and ignorance. All boundaries and limits are in place because of our conditioning (learned responses),

9

and can expand or contract depending upon levels of safety and how willing the person is to commit to experiencing deeper levels of themselves.

If we bend down and try to touch our toes while keeping our knees straight, we will be only able to reach a certain point before we experience tension and stiffness. This measures the extent of our limitation that we can stretch ourselves with those muscles at this point in time. This is one of our boundaries and boundaries are very important places for this edge is our teacher, from which we can learn more about ourselves. Each time we approach this teacher either physically, emotionally, or intellectually, with sensitivity, love, and awareness we will find that the boundary will expand allowing a greater range of movement and experience with each meeting. If, because of our fear or self-sabotage behaviour we withdraw from approaching our limit, our teacher, we will learn nothing new and in time our own physical restrictions, fear, and dogma will contract upon themselves and our world will shrink.

At the physical level when we approach our limits sensibly, with full awareness, the body responds by drawing 'Life Force' energy to that particular area being exercised. This encourages blood and energy to permeate the muscles and organs with nourishment and vitality. Without this stretching experience of touching the outer reaches of our comfort zone, we turn inward and the muscles atrophy, limiting the physical body further.

At the emotional level we approach our limit/teacher by allowing ourselves to feel each emotion as it arises. Many people have the idea that emotions such as anger, fear, or jealousy are bad and "should" be controlled or supressed, and not be experienced. This type of thinking has driven more

10

people insane than any other psychological trauma a person can experience. Feelings are our friends, particularly uncomfortable emotions, for they are valuable teachers in as much as they show us that we are telling ourselves about a particular experience may be incorrect. If I conclude that some experience is bad, such as having an argument with my spouse, this will create a certain energy in me that manifests as an emotion. If I focus on that emotion rather than withdraw my awareness away from it as is the tendency, I will experience an emotional boundary, and expand my ability to feel. The ability to feel love and joy depends upon our ability to feel all emotions, and not just the comfortable ones.

At the Mental level we approach our limit/teacher by observing ourselves impartially. This 'Self-Observing' is not intellectually analysing, or being obsessed with thinking about ourselves all the time, but simply being a silent witness to all that happens, without judgement, opinion, or attachment. Those who engage in self centered reflections (when one identifies with their pain or situation), have a tendency to want to change things, whereby 'Self-Observing' is an act of impartially watching our flow of consciousness in relation to ourselves, our world and all the people that enter into it. We learn through the act of watching without interference, or trying to judge whether something is good or bad, pleasant or unpleasant, right or wrong. Self-Observing enables us to examine the results of our daily actions. If our actions create havoc in our lives, we know that we need to be more aware. This awareness will show us that we may need to accept and then let go of limitations within us, rather than try to change other people or unhappy circumstances in our lives.

Our limit/teacher shows us that we are an integrated fully functioning Spiritual being, and that we are One with all parts of ourselves (physically, emotionally and intellectually), as well as with the rest of the Universe. We may at this stage only experience our limitations and our boundaries, and not our Integrated perfection because our early life experiences may have convinced us that we are limited in some way. Yet, our limit/teacher encourages us to pass through our boundaries and eventually experience our limitlessness, and wholeness, the very Fountainhead of our Divine Self. We stop ourselves from doing this because of our fear and our commitment to our false and mostly unconscious beliefs that tell us we live in a world that has many dangers.

PROTECTIVE BARRIERS AND DEFENSE MECHANISMS:

Protective Barriers are the psychological walls we erect around us to protect us from a perceived hostile and dangerous world. We erect these because we are frightened at the thought of what we believe others can do to us or against us. We each have a frightened, hurt child within us that remembers how it was wounded earlier in life: perhaps during pregancy when we picked up our mother's emotions of feeling unsupported, or unloved or resentment of the child she carried; the traumatic experience of birth, the emotional pain of parental disapproval, and the numerous other experiences that we concluded were traumatic. These all add up to us wanting love and not finding it, and wanting to escape and hide. Protective Barriers are the result of unresolved fears, and so it is not surprising that we erect such barriers to keep ourselves safe within the confines of our comfort zones and keep others who could be threatening at a safe distance.

You know someone else has a Protective Barrier up when you come into their presence. There seems to be a distance, a separation, an imaginary wall between you and them. Communication between you may be superficially polite, but there is an urge to leave or put up a protective barrier of your own. You don't feel completely safe with that person, particularly in sharing your inner most thoughts and feelings with them.

Protective Barriers not only keep others outside, they also keep us trapped inside. They effectively keep us feeling separate from others, the world, from our Source (God), and ultimately from ourselves.

Where Protective Barriers act as a psychological wall, Defense Mechanisms are the behaviours we use to hide behind the barriers. Defensive behaviours such as being critical of others, becoming resentful, or turning on the cold, silent treatment to make someone feel bad. It is important to understand the difference between Protective Barriers and the Defense Mechanisms we use, because we can more readily observe our behaviour rather than our barriers. Barriers are much harder to see, especially our own. In observing our behaviour we will eventually see and get in touch with the Protective Barrier that is limiting us.

Yet, it is not things or other people we defend ourselves against that is the danger, it is the very defense itself that hurts us. When we feel the need to defend ourselves we are feeling frightened, and that fear acts like a magnet which attracts the same kind of energy to itself. It is common knowledge that if you fear an animal such as a ferocious dog, it will probably attack and bite you. If you have no fear and only love for the animal, it soon calms down and becomes friendly. It is the same with every

Protective Barrier we have. It will eventually attract to itself the very thing we fear will happen.

A friend of mine, Paul once told me how he was at a party that was gate crashed by a local gang of 'bikies'. They started to smash the place up and push people about. All the guests were very frightened except for the host, who knew that to show fear would probably escalate the already tense situation. Instead, he approached the leader in a friendly and carefree manner, explaining that the party was a private function, but if he and his fellow gang members would come with him to a room out the back, he would love to give them all a drink before they left. They did, and thirty minutes later, the gang left as good friends and a potentially difficult situation was avoided. The host knew, that if he became frightened (a Defense Mechanism operating) like everyone else, the gang would probably have wrecked the place and the police would have had to be called in.

Rather than serving us contructively, each defense we have, ultimately prevents us from experiencing deeper levels of Joy, Love, and Creative Self-Expression.   Each Protective Barrier and Defense Mechanism is an unresolved fear from the hurt little child within that is crying out for love.

A Protective Barrier is really a fear barrier, that keeps us trapped within our comfort zone. To become free and loving it is vital to first identify each defense that is operating in order to see how our defensive stance no matter how subtle, is blocking off our stream of 'Life Force', while blocking others off from loving us.

I can hear people reading an idea like defenses for the first time asking: "what about defending ourselves against tyrannical governments, aggressive military powers, terrorists attacks, violent criminals, demanding people, manipulating relationship partners?" There are no short answers to such questions and so the rest of this book is dedicated to addressing this issue and leading us to discover the answers deep within ourselves.

Let us explore our Defense Mechanisms and reveal each self-sabotaging behaviour pattern in ourselves. These are some of the main defenses I have observed in myself and in others while working in therapy:

* Playing out different roles for a contrived effect. (Putting on a different mask for the boss, another for subordinates, our children, visitors, our priest/minister, etc.)
* Using criticizism to control or manipulate others.
* Sarcasm to belittle others in order to get our needs met.
* Blaming others because our life isn't working.
* Being aggressive verbally or physically to get our way.
* Being argumentive or resisting other people's viewpoints.
* Cold, silent treatment, to manipulate others to change.
* Subtle attack - Shift the focus of attention from our own personal shortcomings onto what is wrong with our partner.
* Rebelling against authority. Where an authority figure demands we do something, the rebel reacts with an opposite behaviour.
* Being a compulsive helper or advisor.
* Wanting to rescue people from their pain or situation.
* Justifying our actions, thoughts or feelings
* Creating negative situations in our lives, rather than letting others do it to us. (Leaving a relationship before we are left and rejected).
* Being the disciplinarian to control others.

* Using any behaviour that controls other people's behaviour (emotional manipulation etc.)

This list is endless and each behaviour reinforces our belief in limitation and the need to protect ourselves, and the hurt child within.

I discovered the importance of understanding Protective Barriers while working with Margaret Mulqueen, a wholistic nurse and Rebirther Trainer during a Rebirthing Practitioners training course we were running together. Margaret had first introduced the idea of Defense Mechanisms to me a month earlier, and it wasn't long before I had first hand experience of seeing it operating in myself. It happened that I felt annoyed at her for some reason during the training and began to voice my feelings. She responded with encouragement for me to express them. Then she pointed out something I was doing that was counter-productive in my work. I immediately became defensive and wanted to become abusive or withdraw. As I observed myself and shared with her what was happening to me, she shared her feelings of also feeling defensive. At this point, the intense feelings around the issue we were sensitive about totally dissolved. From this honest sharing we both discovered how we were limiting ourselves and reinforcing our fears.

Since that day I have become even more aware of my Protective Barriers and defensive behaviours. As I observe them operating I begin to understand why they are there, why I think I need to defend myself. With this knowledge and as I develop my levels of safety, each barrier begins to dissolve, the Defensive behaviour stops operating, and I begin to feel one with the people in my life. It is a wonderful experience to begin to live without Barriers and Defenses. It is a little frightening at first, but it is a sure ticket to Freedom.

Try this the next time you are feeling any emotion of discomfort while around ot her people. Ask yourself:

* What am I afraid of right now?
* What do I need to defend right now?
* Will I reach understanding and unity with this person if I let go of the need to protect myself?

EXERCISE:

List 10 Defense Mechanisms you use to protect yourself when you feel threatened :

EG * When I get criticised I feel angry.
     * When I feel frightened, I withdraw inside myself.
     * I become sarcastic when no one listens to me.

1. _____
2. _____
3. _____
4. _____
5. _____
6 _____
7. _____
8 _____
9. _____
10 _____

Affirmation:

IT IS SAFE TO LIVE WITHOUT DEFENSES AND FULLY EXPERIENCE ALL ASPECTS OF LIFE!

CHAPTER THREE

BREATH INTEGRATION FORMULA FOR FREEDOM:

In 1988, Jane Davies, a professional Rebirther from the Hawkes Bay, New Zealand, made an interesting discovery. The problem she and other therapists faced, was how to teach people the effectiveness of correct breathing without long and complicated explanations. Certainly, one could simply show them by getting them to do it, but most people want more understanding before they are willing to try something new. One day while Jane was looking at the Five Components of Rebirthing as written in 'Rebirthing Made Easy', she wondered what would happen if she totally reversed the healing process. She jotted down on a piece of paper the reversed process and what stared back at her was the obvious way people create disease and unhappiness in their lives. What was obvious about it, was that as a successful therapist she was very familiar with how people sabotage their lives, but had found it difficult to get the message across to those who needed to hear it the most. What she had written down was a very simple formula for explaining to people how they suppress feelings, and stay stuck. Then by presenting the opposite formula, that of the Five Components, she could show how Integration and healing was easily achieved.

When Jane was next in Auckland, she showed the formula to me, and I couldn't contain my excitement as she began to explain it. Within two minutes I realised as she had, that this formula could be explained to anyone, even without them understanding any form of Breath Healing. We sat together and refined it even further. I finally had the formula I had been searching for for years. I often give thanks to Jane for her commitment to excellence.

* * *

THE FORMULA FOR DISEASE AND UNHAPPINESS:

Think of a nagging problem you have that keeps re-occurring in your life. Perhaps how you are mistreated by your boss, spouse, friends, relative etc. You find yourself in a difficult situation like being threatened by creditors with repossession of property, or whatever.

What do you do in a situation where you find yourself stressed, under pressure, or activated and upset.

Look at the following diagram and start at '1' bottom of the diagram.

SELF DEFEATING CYCLE
Victim state

1. We find ourselves in a situation - that our conditioning (ego) tells us is unpleasant or undesirable.

2. We become more aware of the situation, and how it may affect us.

3. We judge it and conclude that the situation is bad or wrong and begin resisting it. This creates certain feelings in our bodies.

4. To cope with the situation and our feelings, we try to escape or avoid what is happening. One way to do this is to hold the breath which enables us to suppress the feelings, and lose our awareness. As a result of resisting our feelings, this builds tension in the body. This can lead to escapist, addictive behaviour, (overeating, drugs and alcohol abuse, obsessive behaviour, suicide etc).

5. We remain stuck. This reinforces our life pattern of struggle and suffering. We feel helpless and a victim, with no ability to change. We pretend the feelings or situation are not there any more.

Is that how it is for you?

With all the thousands of people I have counselled and worked with over the years as a therapist, I have found that is exactly the way they react to the difficulties in their lives. That is the way I react to life when I'm frightened and not prepared to face an undesirable situation.

The following diagram offers an alternative strategy for reversing the suppressing process and leads to freedom and happiness:

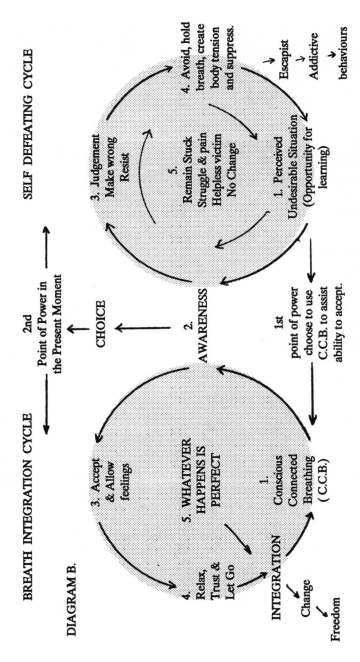

BREATH INTEGRATION CYCLE

SELF DEFEATING CYCLE

DIAGRAM B.

2nd
Point of Power in
the Present Moment

CHOICE

2.
AWARENESS

1st
point of power
choose to use
C.C.B. to assist
ability to accept.

SELF DEFEATING CYCLE:

4. Avoid, hold breath, create body tension and suppress.

→ Escapist
→ Addictive
→ behaviours

5. Remain Stuck Struggle & pain Helpless victim No Change

1. Perceived Undesirable Situation (Opportunity for learning)

3. Judgement Make wrong Resist

BREATH INTEGRATION CYCLE:

3. Accept & Allow feelings

5. WHATEVER HAPPENS IS PERFECT

1. Conscious Connected Breathing (C.C.B.)

4. Relax, Trust & Let Go

INTEGRATION
→ Change
→ Freedom

The left hand circle is the 'Five Components of Breath Integration', and shows us how we can break the limiting 'Self-Defeating Cycle'.

1. CONSCIOUS CONNECTED BREATHING:

When we feel threatened, frightened or in an undesirable situation, we can choose to breath in a Conscious Connected manner (as explained in chapter 5). This is the first point of empowering ourselves to bring us back to the present moment. This has the effect of increasing awareness and more readily accepting the situation as a learning experience, rather than making it wrong, enabling us to move into the left hand circle to Freedom.

2. AWARENESS:

With more awareness, we discover we have more choices. Choice is the mark of freedom, and it reduces stress. This is the second point of empowering ourselves. We discover with awareness that the point of power is in the present moment, and we can either choose to stay with our habitual limiting choices that keep us stuck, or we can use the negative situation as an opportunity to learn from.

3. ACCEPT AND ALLOW THE FEELINGS:

The Breath and Awareness (the first two Components) allow this to happen quite easily. With awareness, we begin to realise that our old strategies are not working. We are now willing to try something new. We accept that our feelings are a natural part of us and that it is O.K. to have these feelings.

4. RELAX, TRUST AND LET GO:

With the Breath, Awareness, and Acceptance (the first three Components), we naturally find it easy to relax, trust and let go. There is no need to struggle and fight against life and Its healing energies.

At this point, Integration often occurs. If not, it is because we are still holding on, making what we are feeling wrong and not accepting and relaxing.

5. WHATEVER HAPPENS IS PERFECT:

The 5th Component is the basis of all the other Components and   is the most important of all, (that is why it is in the centre   of the diagram). This Component allows us to realise that the   existing so-called 'negative' situation is perfect as a learning experience. The strength of the fifth Component is that it teaches us that we don't have to try to make anything happen.   Many systems of learning insist that you must do something, believe in something, put effort in and so on. If   you don't succeed, you must try harder. What this says is   give up all effort and struggle. If you are not succeeding,   then relax more. This is the path of non-striving. If you   study natural law, you will learn that all nature takes the   line of least resistance.

From Rebirthing Made Easy:

"Everything is perfect in the present moment. Therefore, we don't try to integrate anything; we don't need to try to achieve results; we don't even need to try to relax. Trying to achieve some particular result, trying to get somewhere signifies resistance and that we are not accepting our here and now experience.... The first four Components are presented only as effective steps to how Integration can best be achieved. But Reality does not always go along with how things 'should be', even if they are proven. Occasionally Integration will happen when we are controlling our breath, when we have lost our awareness, while finding an experience unpleasant, and possibly even when our muscles are tensed. Rebirthing is one of the safest and simplest techniques we can ever use, and because we don't have to do it right to make it work, it is safe to experiment."

All pain we feel in the body or mind is a signal that we are resisting something - probably resisting experiencing the Truth.

Study the Breath Integration Cycle diagram for a few minutes and see how it works. It is your passport to liberation.

THE FIVE COMPONENTS OF BREATH INTEGRATION:

1. Conscious Connected Breathing.
2. Total Awareness.
3. Accept and Allow the feelings.
4. Relax, Trust and Let Go.
5. Whatever happens is Perfect.

CHAPTER FOUR

INTEGRATION AND INTEGRITY.

Some of our modern day psychological therapies like Rebirthing, Psycho-drama, and Primal Therapy are often regarded by many people as techniques in activation of past suppressed, traumatic experiences. The idea is to bring to the surface of a person's awareness the memories and feelings of the past that keep them trapped in their suffering, and then to release it in an effective manner.

The art of any permanent healing lies not so much in the ability to activate suppressed memories of the past, although this can be an important first step, but in the ability to bring about INTEGRATION in the NOW. Activation is the easy part, and can be brought about by anyone with a little training. The ease of activation can be demonstrated by the fact that if someone came up to you in the street and abused you for no apparant reason, I suspect you would become activated and upset rather quickly. Memories of your lack of self worth would come flooding back to you in the form of fear or anger (fight / flight syndrome). True healing is experienced through the power of Divine Love. This can be greatly helped when a Practitioner effectively uses his or her skills to assist the client to experience this Divine Love and reach Integration for themselves.

What does Integration really mean? I won't attempt to try and answer this monumental question in one chapter, but will spend much of this book addressing this very point. For a start, Integration means to make whole from fragmented parts, and in this context, to bring about a total healing. The fragmented parts being those areas of our lives that are not working, and are creating suffering for us.

To Integrate or to heal something appears to be doing something. In fact it is something that stops happening. The effort to hold on to a limiting belief or a protective barrier ceases and Perfection is allowed to run it's course without interferrence from the ego. The reason a person is emotionally hurting or fearful is because they once formed a limiting conclusion about an experience. They passed a judgement that made that experience bad, wrong or painful, at the intellectual level. In order to feel O.K. again, they withdrew their awareness away from the object of their anger, hurt, or fear, as well as from the feelings themselves. In other words, they dissasociate themselves from what is happening and thus, suppress the whole experience. This is performed on a mental and emotional level. To facilitate this on the physical level, they partly hold their breath. That is why breathing is so important, because it reverses the reaction of supression and helps Integrate the fear as it's happening.

We know we have Integrated a healing when we allow ourselves to become fully aware of an experience we once perceived as bad, wrong or painful, and now choose to accept and enjoy it. The long term effects of Integration are that we no longer get activated by a re-occuring negative situation in our lives.

Debra is a young woman who use to care a lot about how

other people thought towards her. She always found herself becoming defensive or angry whenever she perceived the slightest hint of criticism from anyone. This kept her isolated with her feelings, because she was afraid to confront even her closest friends through fear of being rejected. Her problem, apart from lacking effective verbal skills, was poor self-esteem. After seven breath sessions, she integrated the memory of how she was constantly criticised by her mother as a youngster. She told me later that three days after the session, in front of everyone at a function, three of her friends criticised the way she was raising her youngest child. This normally would have devastated her. Yet, she was able to stay calm and respond that perhaps there were areas she could improve upon, but she felt she was doing OK. She was so excited and feeling so good about herself at the new way she was handling life without the old, automatic fear/anger reaction to other people's criticism. It was alright for others to perceive her negatively, because she had enough awareness and self esteem to choose a new positive response.

Integration happens when we no longer resist that which was bothering us, whether it be a life situation like Debra's experience, or an energy pattern manifesting in the physical body. Either it disappears or we begin to enjoy it.

The main aim of the Breath Integration process is to bring together and make whole the Intellect, the Emotions and the Physical body into an effective and harmonious unit. These three faculties are your functions while here on earth. Those functions are not *you*. They are your instruments or equipment to use while you are here. They are perfectly designed to carry out your every wish, much like a willing slave, although most people don't seem to understand how to use them to their best advantage.

The Intellect, Emotions and the Physical body, although designed to perform separate functions, were ultimately designed to act as one component. This is rarely achieved because of the way people live their lives and the way they think. Certain thoughts - those of a negative nature, originally formed as a result of birth trauma or some other perceived negative experience, create stress in each of the functions causing a separation of the three. Thus, the three functions begin to act independently of each other, creating disharmony. This imbalance causes a person to view life negatively and make further limiting conclusions about life experiences which creates an emotional response called fear. Thus, we erect the mental and emotional protective barriers we talked about in Chapter Two. On the physical level the fear response instructs the muscles in the body to tighten up defensively, and this in turn causes them to burn energy for no constructive purpose; and can continue doing this for a life-time. Neither sleep nor ordinary rest is enough to release this stress. Something else is needed to release the stress and bring about an INTEGRATION. When the three functions are Integrated, ie. working as a harmonious unit, all limitations cease to have meaning, resulting in all parts of the person supporting their aliveness, joy and love.

Yet total Integration is even more than the definition written here, because the Whole is always greater than the sum total of all its parts, just as a person's thoughts are more powerful when concentrating on a single project than when they are scattered over a number of projects at the same time. The individual notes of a piece of music amount to little until they all come together and are heard as a complete symphony. It is the conscious experience of all the different parts together as a single unit THAT sustains the harmony among the parts. When we use our intellect, emotions, and our physical faculties in unison, we create perfect harmony between them.

IT IS CONSCIOUSLY EXPERIENCING THE HARMONY AMONG THE DIFFERENCES THAT IS TRUE INTEGRATION, and also true Spirituality.

All parts of a person are perfect, even when they are not acting in harmony. So the problem is not with the parts themselves, but rather with their function and misuse. People like to categorise and judge things in order to understand and relate to their world. But, this has the problem of limiting their judgement down to what they believe in. For example, a man who believes that his political party is better than every other one, will judge every politician on this view point. So, the question is not whether something is good or bad, right or wrong, , or even better or worse; the question is what works for us one hundred percent of the time. By approaching our 'inner self work' from this point of view rather than from value-judgements, we are able to stay objective, and clear of ego.

What many students of Truth discover as they become more Integrated from the techniques described in this book, is a new love of life. This is because the ego is being Integrated along with the three functions. It is not necessary to get rid of the ego, because, it in fact does not even exist. Ego is simply a figment of the imagination, an illusion. But, if one has a belief that something is bad and has to be eliminated, then this is just another limited thought and probably what started one's stress in the first place. After all, how can you get rid of something that doesn't even exist? Why even talk about it, some people ask. When we forgot who we really were, we stopped believing in our Divinity, and so stopped experiencing universal love and joy. A void was created, much like a lifeless desert in the mind: and suffering became possible. This void became the subconscious mind, a mind of unawareness, a mind filled with frustrations and fears, and all manner of illusions. The part of the subconscious mind being referred to is not the instinctive part, that keeps our body functioning, such as breathing, heart beat and so on. What is being discussed here is the part that creates illusions through negative and limiting thoughts and conclusions about life experiences. It is through this part of the subconscious mind that we have separated ourselves from ourselves through the separation of the three functions, thus having no longer the experience of being connected with our True Selves.

It is often asked at my classes: "Is it the void of the subconscious mind that cause's suffering or the ego's attachments within the subconscious?"

It could be said that the ego within the subconscious mind causes the suffering. Yet, as the ego doesn't exist in reality any more than the void of the subconscious, it doesn't cause suffering except to keep us separated from experiencing our Divine Self on a conscious level. It is because of this separation that we conclude that some of our experiences are suffering. It is a belief in separation that creates an ego which has a need to protect itself from imagined dangers.

The illusory subconscious mind is the home of the illusory ego, and ego is based upon survival, and the fear of non-existence. If a person, fears a part of life or the people in it, the ego can even destroy the physical body through disease and accidents in order to escape from a perceived hostile world. This has been referred to as 'Death Urge'. Of course, it doesn't usually go this far, because the 'Life Urge' is stronger than the 'Death Urge', but it does tend to keep us from experiencing the real joys of life through sickness, unhappy relationships, broken careers, lack of confidence, anxieties, being defensive and so on. Yet all that is necessary to start the process of Integration is to stop believing that shadows are real.

If you are finding some of this confusing at this point, that is alright. We shall address this subject again later.

INTEGRITY:

The word Integration, along with the word Integrity, comes from the Latin word ' *integer*', which means wholeness, and to unify.

Integrity means honesty in the minds of most people, and all agree that honesty is the best policy, being truthful is a great thing, the golden rule, and so on. Yet, most of us are dishonest to ourselves every day: those little self put-downs; that we are not good enough; that we can't get enough of the things we want; and a belief in lack and mediocrity. Most people sell themselves short in how they think, feel and act. The lies we tell others is nothing compared to the lies we tell ourselves. These are what keep us trapped, and the problem is that most of them are unconscious. We give up a portion of our Integrity every time we give our power away to anyone or anything outside of ourselves; every time we stop believing in ourselves.

ENVY:

One of the most crippling behaviours to a person's Integrity lies in the habit of envy. Envy means a grudging contemplation of more fortunate persons. Nine out of ten people engage in some form of this ultimate self put-down.

Envy is based upon the false thought that we cannot create

for ourselves what we see in others, or what others have. When a person becomes successful, everyone acknowledges him, or her, either positively or negatively, depending upon where the acknowledger is coming from - love, or fear.

Benjamin Franklin once wrote:

'Whoever feels pain in hearing a good character of his neighbor, will feel a pleasure in the reverse. All those who despair to rise in distinction by their virtues, are happy if others can be depressed to a level with themselves.'

Here's a story that highlights my point:

In ancient Greece there lived a very prosperous and virtuous man called Aristides. As time passed, many people became jealous of his continued success. It was decided to call for a vote amongst the citizens of Athens to have him ostracised (it was a common practice to banish those regarded as dangerously powerful or over-popular around that time). As Aristides was walking toward the voting place to cast his own vote, he was stopped by an illiterate voter who didn't recognise him and asked if he would mark his tablet in favour of banishment. Aristides asked the man, "What have you against Aristides? What has he done wrong?" The voter replied, "Nothing, but I'm tired of hearing him called 'the Just' ".

It is written in the Proverbs: *'Wrath is cruel, and anger is outrageous, but who is able to stand before jealousy?'*

A person with envy is someone who believes he or she is inferior and who feels resentment against those who appear superior. Of course it is never admitted; and such people have all the answers and smart comments, aimed at demeaning and putting down the person or group to which they feel inferior. It is interesting to note, that monuments have never been built for critics!

The point is, it's not what we or others do, or fail to do, that's important; IT'S HOW WE JUDGE THEM THAT DESTROYS OUR INTEGRITY. Common gossip hurts those who engage in it more than the person being talked about. The north American Indians have a wonderful saying, *'Before you judge a man, walk for two days in his moccasins'.*

As it is written - *'Let he who is without error cast the first stone'.*

In higher awareness we discover that to judge another is impossible. How can we possibly know all that motivates another: what pressures, fears, and reasons for doing things in a particular way. It is ego that assumes it knows the rightness or wrongness of other's actions.

This is not to say that judgement is good or bad, for to say that to judge another is wrong, is just another judgement. To judge another is not wrong, but it can affect the person being judged as well as the person doing it. This is also not saying that we must give up all evaluations of our world, other people and of ourselves. In fact very few of us can do this anyway. Judgements against the actions of others doesn't really serve us constructively, but evaluations do. True evaluations are simply observing impartially with full awareness of all that happens. With such awareness, the appropriate course of action is always clear.

WHOLENESS:

The truth about Integrity is that everyone has it. However, everyone expresses their Integrity in different ways, and sometimes, in ways we don't understand. Rather than be concerned about other people's Integrity, it is more important to be concerned about our own.

Integrity means being one hundred percent honest with ourselves one hundred percent of the time. It is telling the truth about ourselves, our feelings, our thoughts, and our wants in a way that respects the rights of others as well as ourselves. Being committed to self-honesty leads to wholeness and Integration.

We may need to examine our personal commitment to our Integrity. The following statements are not meant to be judgements, but rather an appraisal of how we may be expressing our own Integrity. How we express it depends upon how Integrated we are in terms of compassion, joy, and inner peace

Because of fear and a belief in limitation within an abundant universe some people choose to limit the expression of their Integrity such as:

* The successful businessman who tries to rip off clients.
* The worker who takes that 'perk' from work that no-one knows about.
* The brilliant scientist or artist whose private life is in a mess.
* The inspirational writer or Spiritual teacher who has a successful social life but is unhappy in his or her personal relationships.
* The thief, the murderer, the rapist, the terrorist, are all expressing a desire or a belief about life that may limit their own creative, self expression. We limit ourselves the moment we

judge them, in our secret belief that we are better than them.

Everyone at some level has room to grow and develop their Integrity. Be aware of those who claim to be completely clear. Mostly they are using a protective barrier to cover up some insecurity - the very thing that could free them if they courageously exposed it.

INTEGRITY LIST:
What must we clean up in our lives in order to be whole?

RELATIONSHIPS WITH SELF: Am I being totally honest with myself; loving and respecting myself and my values?

RELATIONSHIPS WITH OTHERS: Do I always tell the truth? Do I engage in gossip? Can others confide in me with safety? Am I open and honest with my feelings and thoughts? Do I respect other's rights and values?

HEALTH: Am I taking care of my body, my mind and emotions? What am I feeding them? Am I inspiring my mind to new heights of achievement, or cluttering it with a stream of violence and trivia through TV and novels? Am I giving my emotions play and love or forming unhealthy attachments? Am I nurturing my physical body with wholesome food and healthy exercise?

ENVIRONMENT: Is my living space clean and tidy, suitable for the Goddess/God within me? Am I contributing to the solutions of Environmental and planetary well-being?

WORK: Am I honest and straight forward with my customers, employer, employees? Am I contributing to the best of my abilities? Am I in the right job for my talents?

FINANCIAL: Do I effectively manage my finances? Am I keeping my agreements to honour my debts? Am I commited to a healthy prosperity awareness, or to lack and poverty?

OTHER: _____

_____

_____

Let us make it our intention to be committed to our own Integrity every day, for it is probably our most valuable asset. Lose our Integrity and there isn't much left to lose. When we discover an area that needs working on, don't feel discouraged. Instead, celebrate that we have found another block that separates us from freedom.

DEVELOPING INTEGRITY:
Integrity involves giving up behaviours that no longer serve us constructively. For example, a child learns very early that by having a tantrum in the supermarket will get him the lollipop. But at the age of 30 or 40, this behaviour won't work, even though he may still be locked-in to the subconscious belief that it will. Throwing tantrums as an adult manifests as creating accidents, illnesses and failing in relationships and careers.

Giving up our self-sabotage behaviours means simply becoming aware of them. The following are areas that trouble most people and have been described as the TWELVE CHIEF FEATURES:

1. SELF REJECTION: Almost everyone walking on the planet has some degree of self hate. A lack of self respect and self love can cause us to hurt our physical bodies and even eventually destroy it through accidents and disease.

2. LIMITING SELF LABELS PREVENTING GROWTH: The affirmations we unconsciously use to reinforce our self rejection such as 'I'm not good enough; It's impossible; I can't get enough; I'm too old; If only...I had done that years ago...'etc.

3. PREJUDICE SYNDROME (VANITY): Prejudging others who appear different from us as being inferior, wrong, or a threat.

4. ANGER AND RESENTMENT: An experience we frequently have when our expectations and demands are not met, and when we give away our power.

5. GUILT AND WORRY: Living outside the present moment, guilt wastes our energy by regretting the past; and worry is fear of the future.

6. JEALOUSY (ENVY): Resenting those whom we think are better than us, and insisting that certain people eg. spouse belong to us. It's being committed to an ownership, or competition mentality.

7. NEED FOR SECURITY: Denying our true inner security in favour of external security such as possessions, money, insurance and retirement funds, power over others, prestige, having someone to love us a certain way, and having someone care for us.

8. HERO WORSHIP: Putting some guru, teacher, lover, singer, actor, etc, on a pedestal and making him or her more important than ourselves.

9. PROCRASTINATION: Frightened of making the wrong choice, or facing up to some situation that involves a decision, which we put it off in the hope that it will go away.

10. BLAMING AND THE 'NOT FAIR' SYNDROME: Demanding that everything be fair and equal, and when it's not, finding someone to blame because our life isn't happy or going as we want it to. Being swept up into self-pity - or the 'POOR ME' Syndrome.

11. THE 'MUSTS, SHOULDS AND OUGHTS' SYNDROME: Not trusting our own decisions and behaviour, and therefore being controlled by conventional rules, laws, and traditions made by someone else that may not serve us.

12. FEAR: Apart from the natural fight-or-flight syndrome, believing in an unsafe universe that is controlled by some power outside ourselves, which will punish us for our wrong thoughts and actions.

Being free of these crippling belief systems will change our world as if we waved a magic wand over it.

* * *

GEMS ALONG THE WAY:

* Integration means to make whole.
* Harmony is achieved when all parts work in unison.
* The whole is greater than the sum total of all its parts.
* The Harmony among the differences is true Integration.
* Be true to yourself and you will be true to all.

CHAPTER FIVE

CONSCIOUS CONNECTED BREATHING THE FIRST COMPONENT

"BREATH OF LIFE"

At the centre of most religious traditions the breath holds an important significance. The word 'Breath' can be traced back to an ancient word that means 'Spirit'. In the Old Testament, it is described that man became a living soul after God breathed His Spirit into him.

Psychology today is just beginning to see a relationship between mental illness and the interruption of the respiratory process as the result of stress. Some therapists are starting to understand what Yoga has known for thousands of years, that harmony and good health are synonymous with correct breathing. Breath therapists, Rebirthers, Yogies and Spiritual Masters are demonstrating that expanded awareness, compassion, and Perfection are realised by un-interrupted respiration.

It has been my observation as a result of conducting thousands of Rebirthing sessions, that most people have some form of damage to their natural breathing mechanism. This is often a result of Birth Trauma.

43

To quote from 'Rebirthing Made Easy':

"As a newborn, nature provides that we receive oxygen through the umbilical cord while learning to breathe in our new environment (having been in fluid for so long), but the custom has been to cut the cord immediately, throwing us into a panic".

At birth our breathing automatically starts, and can take a little time to allow the body to adjust to receiving oxygen for ourselves through the lungs. but as the result of being suddenly severed from our life-support system (our Mother), our need to be breathing correctly was something like a forced start. Either we learnt very quickly to breath, or we died right there at birth. In our panic and desire to live, we took a deep breath, and the air hitting our delicate lungs for the first time produced excruciating pain. Not only did our physical breathing mechanism become damaged, we also associated breathing with pain, (psychologial damage) and our breathing has been shallow ever since, much to the detriment of our health. Most of us were psychologically damaged because it was at this point most of us learned that by controlling the exhale, we could suppress unpleasant feelings and experiences. As we are Divine Beings, it is our nature to want to feel 'happy'. So when we feel anything less than our perfection, we learnt that by controlling our exhale we could suppress our real feelings and start to feel OK. again. Because we have been doing this all our lives, it is so engrained in us as a habit, that we are totally unconscious of how we suppress our feelings.

SUPPRESSION OF AN EXPERIENCE:
1. We are faced with a situation that our conditioning tells us is bad.

44

2. We start to think that this may give us pain, and begin to feel fear.

3. We conclude that this should not be happening, that it is bad or wrong, and resist the situation.

4. Our muscles tighten, and we start to hold or control our breathing.

5. This helps us to withdraw our awareness, ignore what's happening, and give away our power, resulting in a loss of personal choice.

The 'self-defeating' cycle all over again!

If you watch a person experiencing a lot of emotion like fear or anger, you will find that their breathing is very restricted and controlled. That is because they are using the breath to try to suppress their feelings at that point. So, by suppressing the breath, particularly by controlling the exhale, feelings and experiences are suppressed and held in the body. Everytime we suppress something, the breathing becomes even more controlled, inhibited and shallow. This is necessary to maintain the suppressed 'Life Urge' at a subconscious level.

The problem with suppressing anything is that the energy has to go somewhere, and it normally settles in the muscles of the body. If you feel deeply into the muscles across your shoulders and the back of the neck, you may find 'sore' spots . These 'blocks' known as muscle spasms are burning energy constantly and that is why people feel drained, lacking in energy and rundown. Imagine how you would feel after all the energy blocks had been breathed out!

Most people while breathing normally have a slight pause or gap between the inhale and the exhale. This is because over the years we have learnt to maintain our suppressions at a manageable level, where they remain in the subconscious without us being aware of them. If we start to connect the inhale and the exhale together in a complete breathing cycle as we do in Conscious Connected Breathing, the energy that is constantly being used to hold our suppressions in place is removed, by the breath. This allows the feelings, and sensations which have been held as suppressed energy in our subconscious to surface up to our conscious mind, where it can be gently released.

Conscious Connected Breathing reverses the suppressing process, allowing the energy to be Integrated in a natural way.

METAPHYSICS OF BREATHING:

INHALE: -
We begin life in this sphere of existence on the Inhale, and every time we breathe in it confirms our individuality. The Inhale is our connection with Truth (the Life Force). It represents life, positive, yang, growth, the sun, and the male aspect within the duality of this plane of existence.

It connects our outer physical respiratory system with our inner Life Force or Prana. It is a direct link between our physical world, and our Higher Spiritual SELF.

EXHALE: -
We end our life in this sphere of existence on the Exhale, and every time we breathe out it confirms our connection with all existence. The Exhale is our elimination process of all that is not in harmony with life. It represents death, negative, yin, the moon, and the female aspect.

It releases all negative, tense, contracted, obstructed, and impure conditions of body, emotions and intellect. This is not surprising when you consider that 70% of all physical elimination of human waste is through the breath.

HIGHER CONSCIOUSNESS:
Higher consciousness is that part of us which is aware of our intellectual, emotional and physical functions, including our breathing and all that enters the mind as the result of correct breathing. Higher Consciousness is the non-judgemental part of us. It concludes nothing, it judges nothing as being good or bad, right or wrong. It simply observes and accepts all without opinion. It has been described in some traditions as the 'Silent Witness', and the 'I AM' principle. This is the part of us which is really the True Self, and in this aspect, it is really All of us. It is All that is real.

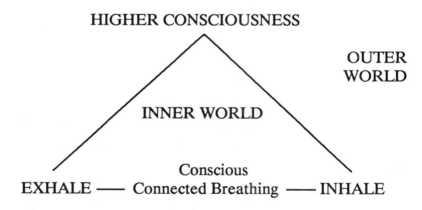

HIGHER CONSCIOUSNESS

OUTER WORLD

INNER WORLD

Conscious
EXHALE —— Connected Breathing —— INHALE

Together with Higher Consciousness, the INHALE and EXHALE create balance and harmony between our Inner and Outer Worlds. This simple process of breathing 'IN' and breathing 'OUT' in a connected, relaxed, method cleanses the aura, balances the chakras, re-aligns the meridians, eliminates waste,

47

and enlivens and heals the entire Being.

By consciously breathing in, we breath in LOVE, HAR-
MONY, and LIFE. By consciously breathing out, we breath out
FEAR, DISEASE and DEATH. Connecting the Inhale with the
Exhale balances the breathing process creating perfect harmony
throughout the whole being.

EXHALE TELLS US HOW PEOPLE LIVE THEIR LIVES:
By observing the exhale of a person, can tell you a lot about
their personal life.

CONTROLLING EXHALE - Represents fear of letting
go, fear of surrendering to a loving world. The belief is that love
and life might be dangerous. The hurt child inside still remembers how it was hurt at birth, and that it's first experience of life
was *painful* and *dangerous*. If at some level of their being, they
equate life with love, which it is, then they could conclude that
life and love is always *painful* and *dangerous*. Controlling the
exhale can also be the result of believing that life and love is
limited in some way. Thus, they try to hold on to what little love
they have in their world, and fear losing even that, which
suppresses not only their Life Urge, but also their feelings and
expression of love even further. This person tends to use sleep
or drugs as an escape from their misery.

PUSHING ON EXHALE - Represents trying to get rid of
something they think is bad. It's pushing life and love away and
a kind of wanting to get it all over with, as soon as possible type
reaction. This person is normally into struggle and making life
hard for themselves.

These two types of breathers, and most of us fit into one

type or the other, become more obvious in a breathing session. The full gentle inhale with a totally relaxed exhale releases the ego and its fear of life from the body and the mind.

THE THREE TYPES OF CONSCIOUS CONNECTED BREATHING IN A BREATH INTEGRATION SESSION:

1. FULL AND SLOW. For activating suppressions. This breath is used to start a session, and also mostly used throughout the process.

2. FAST AND FULL. For regaining consciousness if feeling sleepy during the session.

3. FAST AND SHALLOW. For lessening intensity of energy patterns, and speeds up Integration by helping to bring the suppressed pattern to a climax:

WHAT A BREATH SESSION IS LIKE:

To obtain the maximin benefit from a Breath Integration, or Rebirthing session, it is best to work with a qualified Practitioner. This has the effect of allowing the process to happen in an environment of safety and love. If you try it on your own, probably nothing much will happen. This is because as suppressed material begins to surface, the unconscious automatic suppressing mechanism will immediately 'stuff' it down again. If a pattern does manage to come up, you may not have the skills necessary to integrate it, which could leave you feeling a little anxious or uncomfortable for a day or two, until the pattern slides back into suppression.

A typical breath session begins by sharing with your Practitioner what has been happening in your life and what you would like to change. Then you usually lie down and breathe in the connected rhythm, coached and gently guided with lots of loving support. The Practitioner reminds you to breathe when negative associations are activated, cause you to hold your breath. After the cycle of activation and Integration is complete, you relax into a peaceful state, after which there is time to discuss any questions raised by the session. An average session lasts for about two hours, which includes about one to one and a half hours of breathing, or what ever is appropriate for that session.

For further information on Conscious Connected Breathing, read 'Rebirthing Made Easy', which goes into greater detail.

The need to breath correctly has never been greater with the levels of stress in our modern world increasing. This is highlighted by the fact that suppression is a way of life. We feel upset over an intense traumatic experience and we are put on tranquilisers which work on calming the mind as well as the muscles, by suppressing their function. We have a headache, so we take a pain killer which suppresses the pain. This often suppresses the symptoms rather than heals them. The point is that we haven't learnt to listen to the important messages the body is telling us. We are so separated from our feelings and physical sensations, we have lost the ability to interpret our inner expressions. Our protective barriers and defense mechanisms are really our suppressing mechanisms which act to desensitise our awareness of our being. When there is an imbalance in the system we experience energy in our bodies as feelings, emotions, or physical sensations of *'pain'*, and these signals are beckoning our awareness to that area which needs our attention. It is power of awareness in the present moment that is the great healer. But we ignore it, shut off awareness and take a pain killer. Symptoms of disease are in fact the start of a healing process. A negative feeling, formally suppressed, is trying to be released and healed. Breath Integration is all about healing the causes as well as symptoms.

REALITY VS. CONCLUSIONS:

The type of birth we had, whether it was traumatic or not, or how we were treated is less important than how we responded to birth as a new born child. In other words, the reality of what is happening to us is less important than what we conclude about what is happening. Our judgements and conclusions are controlled by the ego which sees only what it wants too. For example, if you were walking along the road one dark night, and suddenly you saw ahead of you the shape of a man with a drawn knife, you would probably become frightened. But, on cautiously approaching you realised that the object was only a bush, your fear would leave you, even though the effects of the fear would remain for some minutes after. Thus, how we respond to things is far more important than what is actually happening. The reason for this is, the subconscious mind cannot tell the difference between reality and perceived reality which can sometimes be illusion. Understanding that our conclusions about life is more important than reality has enormous possibilities in healing and personal growth.

A man had an incurable disease, and was told by his doctor that he had about six months to live. Some months later, while living out the remainder of his life on a distant South Pacific Island, and with his health deteriorating, there was a mix up in the Doctors filing system. Somehow, the mans file got mixed up with someone else's, and on inspection, the Doctor became convinced that the dying man had been mis-diagnosed, and was instead healthy. He sent a message to his patient that he was not going to die after all and to return for further tests. The dying man was overjoyed at his reprieve and due to his isolation, he was unable to return until a month later. By the time he did return, his health had been nearly restored, and the tests proved it. Soon after, the mix-up was discovered, and his original file showed that he should nearly be dead. The miracle cure baffled the Doctor, who did not understand the healing power of the mind; did not understand that the immune system has a direct relationship to the belief system.

This story is fictitious of course, but it is based upon the numerous 'unexplained' healings, witnessed by Breath Therapists, when their client's have let go of a limiting belief.

The New Growth revolution that is quickly expanding, is very closely connected with consciously using mind-power, and the 'Spirit' of breathing. When we understand the breath we see that we keep unconsciously interferring with a natural process that works perfectly well on its own. Our fear is supported by an over-controlled breathing pattern, which acts to close off our awareness, and also limits the power of the mind. As we become clear and Integrate our over-sized egos, the new expanded consciousness allows us to see that the breath is the path Home, back to Ourselves.

The words 'Breath Integration', implies that Integration and healing are achieved through breathing, and this is largely true. However, Integration happens more effectively when one has a sense of ease and safety, and this is better achieved with the combination of all the 'Five Components'.

CHAPTER SIX

HIGHER CONSCIOUSNESS THE SECOND COMPONENT

The key to Integration lies in the ability to be Present in the moment.

It is a common belief that the past is the key to one's future, and for most, this is a fair comment. A person who's thoughts are predominantly focused upon the past will create a future of similar consequence. But there is another aspect which over-rides all that has happened in the past, and that is the Present Moment.

THE PRESENT MOMENT
The Present moment is all there is. The point of an individuals personal power is right NOW. Nothing else exists except in memory of the past, or expectation of the future, which are only illusions in the here and now.

All our experiences from the past is important for success in any endevour, but when compared with the PRESENT MOMENT, it is over-rated, and interestingly enough, usually by people commited to personal failure. You can listen for hours in pubs and bars as people, half drunk, unhappy in their jobs and relationships recount all the experience they have had, and all that they have done.

The past is where we picked up all our negative conditioning and beliefs, as well as our positive ones. But just imagine for a moment, if we lived only in the PRESENT MOMENT, with no referrance to the past, I imagine that life would be total Bliss and Love. To be free of nagging worries, fears, guilts, and resentments, which all relate to a time other than now would be wonderful. But, what does living in the now really mean?

I remember one fine Winter afternoon, I was walking along a bush track, beside a small stream, lost in my usual mass of thoughts, unaware of my surroundings except for a vagueness of where I was, and what I was doing. Suddenly, the bank gave way and I found myself sitting in the middle of the stream with the water up to my chest, and very conscious of how cold the water was. I became aware that only seconds ago I was lost in the hypnotic trance of thoughts which had no relevance to what was happening now. It had taken a near accident to jolt me back to the present. As I sat there, observing my surroundings, the temperature of the water, the wet clothes against my skin, I had this amazing sense of pure awareness. It wasn't like I was thinking "I am aware", or I'm sitting in a stream freezing. It was suddenly being free from the attachment of thought.

This had occurred to me another time when I was on a beach years before, when I had noticed that the roar of the ocean had seemed to wash away all my thoughts. What I experienced then on that beach was what I was experiencing now, such a feeling of peace, clarity, and of being one with myself. Such a moment is the essence of true awareness and in a way a living meditation.

What this taught me was that when awareness is identified with a thought, we only exist in a certain space and time dimension. The awareness seems to be controlled by the thought, which is in turn controlled by one's early life conditioning (ego). But, when awareness goes beyond thought, we are able to break free of the limitations of time and space. In that instant we are able to observe thoughts coming and going as they pass through the mind without attaching themselves to any other thought already there. And as the awareness becomes even freer in this instant, we begin to see the space between the thoughts, and what we see is eternity and our liberation.

Such a rare experience reveals how mechanical we are and how little we really experience the Present Moment. This also shows that the ego can only exist outside the Present Moment. When we leave the sanctuary of the now can we be controlled by the ego, and all the thought forms associated with it.

'The ego is a prisoner of time, but as we come into the Present Moment we are released from our attachments and anxieties, freed from our past and our future and liberated from our ego. The present moment gives us perfect freedom from our 'conditioned ego.' - Rebirthing Made Easy, P.35.

It seems that the human race is in a form of psychic sleep, lost in a multitude of thoughts, feelings and actions, yet never totally present except in times when one is jolted back through accident or near disaster. Life is more of a dream than a reality, from which only a few seem to awaken. So deep is the hypnotic slumber that humans do their daily jobs, walking, talking, making laws, doing business, making love and raising families in a haze of sleeping awareness. The actions are mechanical and automatic, and depend upon the programmes instilled by years of conditioning through education, religious, and political indoctrations, and the beliefs passed on from parents.

Higher Consciousness is experienced by expanding awareness beyond thoughts, feelings and beliefs, and to know the inner chambers of 'The True Self', which is Truth, Love, and Perfection.

Memory, although linked to conditioning (ego) is quite separate from it. A person living outside the Present Moment for most of the time, either in the past or the future is controlled by the automatic reflex action of conditioning. Yet, the person living predominantly in the Present Moment is free from the effects of conditioning, but still has memory. A master like the Buddha, Christ, or Krishna, who were clear of ego, could still remember names of people and places as well as other useful information within memory.

There are Two types of Time:
1. Earth time is measured by clock, calendar, and the movement of the planets around the sun.
2. Spiritual time is immeasurable because there are no minutes, days, years, past or future.

THE ETERNAL NOW
NOW always exists. NOW always IS. NOW is all there IS.

PAST <--------------- NOW --------------> FUTURE

'The Present Moment is perfect bliss. It is impossible to suffer or be unhappy in the Present Moment. Consider this. The next time you are feeling unhappy, look closely and you will see how it is linked to something that has already happened in the past, or something you think will happen in the future. If you are unhappy with a present existing situation, it is because you are comparing it with a memory of a more pleasant past experience, or with a

hopeful expectation of the future.' Rebirthing Made Easy, P18.

Psychosomatic illness of every kind springs from the pressure of living in a different time span to NOW. Every hospital, prison and mental institution could be emptied in a week if those suffering human beings could understand this secret. The PRESENT MOMENT holds the key to all healing, all freedom, all salvation. From the PRESENT MOMENT flows LIFE, LOVE and WISDOM.

While we continue to attach ourselves to the illusions of negative thought forms we remain controlled by the ego, and this may cause us to be filling our lives with avoidance behaviours, which we use to distract ourselves from Reality.

WHAT IS MY ESCAPE FROM REALITY?
Ask your self this: 'What chemicals do I use, or activities do I engage in to escape from a perceived hostile and unpleasant world'?

In the early part of my adult life, I used alcohol, caffeine and nicotine, as my escape. I found that by habitually using these drugs I did not feel my emotions, emotions I didn't trust. I was afraid to feel. As I got into personal growth work, I replaced these addictions with a set of new ones. Every time I started feeling unhappy due to my unwillingness to face some issue that was happening in my life at that point, I would find my nose in some 'self-improvement' book. Yes, people even use postive things to keep themselves asleep. I read hundreds of such books, and all the time kidding myself that I was really in touch with myself and life. I discovered after years of this avoidance behaviour that, even though I had a large amount of knowledge about spirituality, I was no further a head in a spiritual sense.

I hadn't done the inner work, and was simply attempting to satisfy an inner hunger with an outer means. This never works.

Here is a powerful exercise that can open up hidden areas of the subconscious mind. Write down the first thing that comes into your mind as you read each question. This is an intuitive exercise and not intellectual.

WHO AM I EXERCISE

WHO AM I?

WHAT AM I?

WHY AM I?

WHERE HAVE I COME FROM?

WHERE AM I GOING?

WHAT IS THIS CREATION I FIND MYSELF IN?

WHAT PART IN THIS CREATION DO I PLAY?

AM I LIVING THIS LIFE AS I WANT TO?

DO I LIVE MY LIFE AS OTHERS SAY I SHOULD?

WHAT MAKES ME HAPPY?

WHAT MATERIAL POSSESSIONS ARE IMPORTANT TO ACCUMULATE?

IS APPROVAL FROM OTHERS IMPORTANT TO ME, and IF SO, WHY?

WHAT CAME UP FOR ME DURING THIS EXERCISE?

Doing this exercise is more important than what you conclude about yourself. Such questions are rarely considered. By doing so, we can open up to Higher Consciousness. Do this exercise again in two weeks time and note any different answers.

* * *

THE 'I AM' PRINCIPLE:

The 'I AM' Principle is a statement which says: "I AM" that "I AM". Nothing else added to that statement is necessary or true.

'I AM' is to acknowledge that I exist, it is the only Reality, and it is the True Self. To add anything after 'I AM' such as "I am happy, or sad, angry, or I am a therapist, a plumber, a Mother, is untrue.

These are the things we do; our function. Function is nothing more than the roles we play, and not to be confused with what we really are.

Most people identify themselves with their functions, yet the moment you add any thing after 'I AM', you are no longer discussing Reality, but simply an extention of reality. The same way as a spade is an extention of the gardeners hands, and not the gardener. That we confuse what we do with who we are is not surprising, considering even very realiable sources of information appear to have added to this delema by confusing the 'I AM' with our function.

The Bible for instance, in JOHN 14: 6, it is written:
"I AM the way, the Truth and the Life. No man approaches the Father except through Me". This has confused Christians and would-be Christians for thousands of years. Christ was a universal figure for the liberation of all humankind, and he was talking about the 'I AM' Principle and the three functions, and not setting up one exclusive group of people to be the only ones able to reach the Father (Self Realisation). How does this relate to the True Self and the three functions?

I AM THE:

INTELLECT (Thinking Function)	= Way
EMOTIONS (Feeling Function)	= Truth
PHYSICAL BODY (Moving Function)	= Life

Through the Intellect is the 'Way', which begins the search for Truth. It is through knowledge, reason and thinking that gives us direction to move towards Integration. (In the west, many of us have over-developed this faculty at the expense of our two other functions).

The Emotions are described as the understanding and the love for 'Truth'.

The Physical body is the container of the 'Life Force', and generates the movement of growth towards higher levels of life and understanding, through the love of life.

Christ taught that the three functions need to be Integrated and working together harmoniously in order for the spiritual aspect to be realised within a human being, and in his terminology, reach the Father. But when one function tries to do the work of another function, the individual becomes divided against him/herself. For example, when the intellect tries to do the work of the emotions, the individual becomes unfeeling and cruel. When the emotions try to do the work of the intellect, judgement and reason become confused. When the Physical (Moving Function) tries to do the work of the intellect, the person falls under the control of habit. Positive conditioning, such as learning a new skill is closely connected to the 'Creative Mind', and is governed by the Intellect until the Physical Function has had enough practice to do it on it's own. But when the Physical (Moving Centre) takes on a new practice without the guidance of the Intellect, such as escapist behaviour for whatever reason, unhealthy, addictive habits are formed, like drug abuse, over-eating, and suppression of feelings.

The role of the Thinking Function is to direct the individual towards higher thought. If another function interfers, the person experiences loss of awareness, inner conversations, imaginings which lead to a dream like mechanical state. In other words, the Thinking function is used to day-dream, worry or resent some other person or situation.

The role of the Feeling Function is to put the person in touch with the higher feelings of love, peace, and joy. If another function tries to interfere, the person attaches him or herself to the pendulum swings in feelings of excitement, and fear, elation, and depression.

The role of the Moving Function is not only to provide a vehicle for the two other centres and keep them balanced, but to also enable us to experience the glory of this physical plane of existence.

The 'I AM' can only exist consciously in the Present Moment. When daydreaming, worrying or resenting someone, the True Self (I AM) goes to sleep. Gurdjieff described human-kind's dilemma of psychic sleep with the following example:

He described the Intellect as the driver of a carriage. The Emotions as the horse that pulled the carriage, and the Physical body as the carriage itself. The Master (the I AM) is the passenger asleep in the carriage. The Master is asleep because of the lack of co-ordination between the three functions. As a result of no instructions from the Master (Inspiration, Creative Imagination, Intuition), the driver (Intellect) fails to direct or control the horse. The horse (Emotions) runs out of control, off the road and over bumps, rocks and hills much to the detriment of the carriage, which most often is eventually destroyed (through accidents and disease of the physical body). But when we enter the glory of the present moment, the Master begins to awaken and order, and peace and perfect direction is restored. I expand these ideas further in the book 'Gurdjieff for Today', which will be published at a later date.

Whether the Master/Mistress (True Self) is asleep or that our consciousness is simply not in touch with Higher Consciousness, is anyone's guess, but the fact remains that most of us are not experiencing It, and probably not even experiencing much else!

Awareness is the key to becoming more alive and knowing the joy of experience. Yet, society is based upon suppressing feelings of pain, negative emotions, and building defense barriers. Our healing depends upon our ability to feel these things. Only then can we use the feelings to Integrate into the wholeness of the Self, and experience our completeness.

CHAPTER SEVEN

TOTAL ACCEPTANCE
THE THIRD COMPONENT

THE MEANING OF TOTAL ACCEPTANCE:

Total Acceptance means recognising the perfection of everything. It is a state of consciousness of non-judgement, and probably one of the most challenging principles for people to accept. It is ironic that the path to eternal joy, love and perfection, is synonymous with non-judgemental acceptance, and yet, is so rarely tolerated. This principle can be best summed up in a beautiful story written by Lao Tzu in ancient China.

'There was an old man in a village, and he was very poor, but even Kings were jealous of him because he had a beautiful white horse. Such a horse had never been seen before because of its magnificent beauty, strength, and pure whiteness. Noblemen and even Kings offered fabulous prices for the horse. But the old man would say "This horse is not a horse to me. He is a person, and how can you sell a person? He is a friend, not a possession. How can you sell a friend? No, it is not possible." The man was poor and there was every temptation, but he never sold the horse.

One morning he discovered that the horse was not in the stable. The whole village gathered and they said, "Foolish old man! We knew it before-hand, that some day the horse would be stolen; and you are so poor! How could you protect such a precious thing?

It would have been better to sell it. You could have fetched any price you asked, any fancy price was possible. Now the horse is gone. It is a curse, a misfortune!"

The old man said "No, wait. Simply say that the horse is not in the stable. This is the fact; everything else is a judgement. Whether it is misfortune or not, how do you know...how can you judge?" The people said, "Don't try to fool us! We may not be great philosophers but no philosophy is needed. It is a simple fact that a treasure has been lost, and it is a misfortune."

The old man said, "I will stick to the fact that the stable is empty and the horse is gone. Anything else I don't know. I don't know whether it is a misfortune or a blessing, because this is just a fragment. Who knows what is going to follow?"

The people laughed, and thought the old man had gone mad. They always knew that he was a little crazy, otherwise he would have sold the horse and lived in riches. But he was living as a woodcutter, and he was very old and still cutting and bringing wood from the forest to sell. He was living hand-to-mouth, and in poverty. Now it was completely certain that this man was crazy.

After fifteen days, the horse returned. He had not been stolen. He had escaped to the wilderness, and not only had he come back, but he had brought a dozen wild horses with him. Again the people gathered and they said, "Old man, you were right and we were wrong. It was not a misfortune. It proved to be a blessing. We are sorry that we insisted."

The old man said, "Again you are going too far! Just say that the horse is back, and say that twelve horses have come with the horse, but don't judge. Who knows whether it is a blessing or not?

It is only a fragment ... unless you know the whole story, how can you judge? You read one page of a book, how can you judge the whole book? You read a sentence in a page, how can you judge the whole page? You read a single word in a sentence, how can you judge the whole sentence? Life is so vast. A fragment of a sentence, and you have judged the whole. Don't say that this is a blessing - nobody knows. And I am happy in my non-judgement."

This time the people could not say much; maybe the old man was again right. So they kept silent, but inside they knew well that he was wrong. Twelve beautiful horses had come back with the white horse. A little training and they could all be sold, and would fetch much money. The old man had a young son, an only son. The young son started to train the wild horses; a week later he fell from one of them and his legs were broken. The people gathered again, and people are people everywhere; again they judged, as judgement comes so easily.

The old man said, "You are obsessed with values! Say only that my son has broken his legs. Who knows whether this is a misfortune or a blessing? Nobody knows. Again a fragment, and all is never given to you. Life comes in fragments and to judge the part is to assume you know the total."

After a few weeks the country went to war with a neighbouring country and all the young men of the town were forcibly taken for the military. Only the old man's son was left because he was crippled. The people gathered crying and weeping, because from every house young people were being taken away. And there was little chance of their coming back, because the country that had attacked was powerful, and the war was being lost. They would probably all die.

The whole town was crying and weeping and they came to the old man and they said, "You were right, old man. God knows you were right! This proved a blessing. Maybe your son is crippled, but still he is with you. Our sons are gone forever! At least he is alive, and with you. And by and by he will start walking. Maybe a little limp will be left, but he will be okay."

The old man again said, "It is impossible to talk to you people. You go on and on - judging and judging. Only say this, that your sons have been forced to enter into the military, and my son has not been forced. But nobody knows whether it is a blessing or a misfortune! Nobody will ever be able to know it! Only God knows."

To judge is to prevent us from becoming one with the total. To judge is to ultimately condemn ourselves to our limitations, and with fragments we become obsessed with small things and jump to conclusions. To judge is to stop growing, but we judge because we can only see a small part.

In the journey of life, as one path ends, another begins; as one door closes, an other opens. We reach a mountain top and a higher mountain is always there. Spirituality is an endless journey. Only those who are not weighed down with dogma, and elaborate belief systems, content with the journey, content just to live the moment and grow into it, are able to walk with the total.

The question is often asked in my classes; Can a person in great pain overcome suffering through non-judgement?

NO COMPARISONS:

Suffering and pain are just patterns of energy which some-one has labelled as bad, and therefore, according to them, should be avoided. Energy just is! If someone cuts their hand, they feel energy. This is a signal from the brain, to pay attention to the damaged area and stop the flow of blood. By paying attention to their hand the healing process begins. But, most people it seems are quick to judge such an event as bad. Here is a great secret to eliminate suffering forever:

Suffering is only possible when we compare one experi-ence with another. For example: If I bump my toe against a rock, I will feel energy. But if I judge that energy as bad, the energy changes into a conditioned belief, with the reaction of 'pain', and thus suffering. Suffering is a perception of mind, and the word 'pain' is a conditioned belief in the minds of most people, of something that is bad. The word 'pain' was invented by confused people who regarded energy as something that was to be avoided. So, if I remove all reference points of comparison, such as comparing my bumped toe with the time before I bumped it, and stay in the present moment, I will certainly feel the energy, but I no longer suffer from it. The idea is to not compare any present moment experience with any other experience. When we let go of comparing, judging and hating, suffering ceases to have meaning and we simply are aware of the energy in the toe.

When I returned to New Zealand after spending two years in the tropics, I found the water around New Zealand too cold, so I gave up swimming in the sea. When I began training as a Rebirther, it was part of the course to be rebirthed in very cold water, and it was in the middle of winter. We had to be immersed in the cold water an inch at a time, which was designed to activate fear, and let me tell you, it worked... I was terrified! After several attempts in which I had to be lifted out of the water paralyzed with fear, I finally overcame it. I breathed into it, and discovered that by concentrating solely upon the feelings, and not comparing the experience with a time when I wasn't in the cold water, I became aware of the intense energy, but it was not unpleasant anymore. All my conditioning was telling me this was too cold and painful. However when I brought my self completely into the present moment, and stopped judging and comparing, I was no longer controlled by the conditioning. I was free in that moment, and here I was enjoying something I once found intolerable. The cold water was actually pleasurable...... WHAT A WONDERFUL DISCOVERY!

Our conditioning, that is our learned responses, cause us to suffer. By comparing any experience only to itself, we can choose to make that experience a pleasant and exciting one. By staying in the here-and-now we remove all reference points to the past and future, and the ego that once told us something was bad, ceases to exist. It works like magic! Thus we can enjoy any experience when we want to. Yes, we can banish suffering from our lives forever, and experience the true meaning of 'Bliss'.

'Pain' or 'pleasure' is only our interpretation. It is possible to change our state of consciousness to one in which we interpret every momentary experience as providing total joy. When we develop beyond the duality of good and bad, pleasant and unpleasant, like and dislike, right and wrong, we will discover that fun and 'pain' are all the same. Every moment we live in the here-and-now means we are being truthful to Reality, and there is no greater inspiration, nor greater Spirituality.

THE CONSTANT STATE OF BLISS:

Pain and struggle have no value other than to make us aware that our thinking is false. If we are into pain and struggle then we may need to change our thinking. This will change our attitude and our belief in suffering, and therefore allow us to experience joy. As a first step, consider this simple and yet magnificent idea which is the philosophical theme running through this entire book. This is it:

We are already in a perfect state of bliss, whether we are aware of it or not.

Isn't that one of the most amazing things you have ever read? When I first learnt this principle that the true part of myself is constantly joyful, I spent two weeks trying to disprove it. After many mental gymnastics and much contemplation, I realized the power of the True Self, which I had been contributing to my ego.

This principle means that even though our inner True Self experiences Bliss all the time, the mind and body don't always perceive things this way. That is because the mind, which controls the body, is itself controlled by early childhood conditioning. Our ego acts like a filter which examines each incoming impression and experience, and judges them according to the predominant set of rules, beliefs and defenses held in the subconscious. Thus the mind looks at life through the ego, much like looking out of a window while it's raining, and the wet glass makes the world appear blurred and distorted. We might be fooled into believing that this is how the world really is. When it stops raining again we can see with clarity. It is the same with the way we perceive life. When we remove the filters from the mind we expand our awareness of the truth. A Self-Realized person is non judgemental, because they are clear of the binding clutches of such an ego. "Know the truth and it will set you free".

WE ARE NOT OUR SUFFERING:

If we accept as a possibility that we are perfect - which the True Self is, though we may not consciously know it as yet - we can begin to see how *thinking* that *we are not perfect* creates conflict in the mind. This is because you cannot have Truth and falseness in the same place at the same time, any more than you can have light and darkness at the same time. They are completely incompatible. When we 'try' to live out of harmony with truth, a conflict begins between our True Self and the illusionary false self, (or ego). This conflict in the mind causes the body to tense up, creating stress. Negative thinking limits our perception and understanding, the same way as if we continually walked around in a very dense fog. Every time we think a false thought, such as 'I'm not good enough', because of its false nature, it eventually leads to suffering. Any thought that is contrary to what we ARE will create disharmony in the mind, and the stress we feel in the body is the result of suppressing those feelings. Every pattern of energy that we experience as uncomfortable in the body is an indication that we are resisting the expression of the Life Force within us.

Most people believe that their suffering is real, as if it were a part of themselves. They identify themselves with their suffering, because their belief in pain is true for them. It is true that feelings are real, because they are actual experiences, yet, they are mostly based upon the illusions of deeply held beliefs.

Here is a valuable technique that will demonstrate this to you, and it can change your life if you practice it: - Every time you start feeling angry, frightened, or sorry for yourself, or having any emotion that makes you feel limited, begin to see those feelings as belonging to you but not being You. They are not the real You. Every time you say to yourself "I'm feeling sorry for myself, I'm feeling angry, I'm feeling frightened", you are in fact lying to yourself, with the result of reinforcing that limiting behaviour. Instead, at such times, begin to separate the falseness from the Truth. Say instead:

I'm feeling beautiful, but 'it's' feeling angry, or 'it's' feeling frightened, or 'it's' feeling sorry for itself". Begin to assign those feelings to where they belong - to the 'ego'. Only the ego has the ability to feel separated and limited. That is why the True Self is incapable of feeling anything other than Bliss, Love and Perfection.

You see, you no longer have an excuse to ever feel unhappy again, as long as you see the games your ego is playing.

The fact is we are experiencing bliss all the time, because that is what we are. But through our ignoring of the Truth we effectively block its flow to our surface consciousness. For example, imagine two magnets which are naturally attracted to each other. If I place a piece of lead between the two of them, the attraction becomes blocked. It is the same with our Inner Perfection; our body and mind are naturally attracted to bliss. They are in fact connected, but if I place an untruthful thought in my mind, and believe in it, I break the connection and the attraction between my body-mind and my true self, becomes blocked. This is why we do not experience Bliss on the conscious level of mind. We have separated ourselves from ourselves by the untruths we believe in.

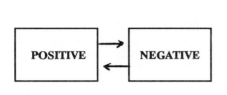

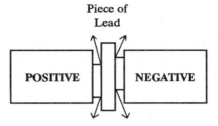

Two magnets have a natural attraction for each other. It is the same with our three functions (intellect, emotions, and physical body) and that of our True Self. They can in fact be integrated as one unit as below.

If a piece of lead is put between the two magnets the attraction is blocked, the same as if stress is lodged in the system through false thinking as below.

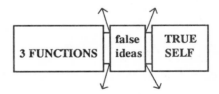

No matter what the mind, the emotions or the body are experiencing, the Inner True Self is in a state of Bliss. When the three functions are fully Integrated with the True Self, Bliss is naturally experienced in the conscious mind.

CHAPTER EIGHT

THE ART OF SURRENDER: THE FOURTH COMPONENT

All my training in stress management has taught me a very important thing, and that is, the most effective way to release tension from the body, is to first give the person permission to relax. The easiest method to bring about Integration is through relaxation. In fact, relaxation is the key to Integration.

Relaxing, like Integration isn't something you do, it's ceasing to tense the muscles of the body. It's simply letting go. Christians have a beautiful saying: 'Let go let God.'

A friend once asked me to describe exactly what relaxation is and how it is achieved, other than just relaxing the muscles of the body. It's all very well telling a highly stressed person to relax, and probably quite ridiculous to expect them to be able to do so. The word that immediately sprang to mind was 'surrender'. I personally had a problem with the word surrender on first being introduced to these ideas. Being an ex-soldier, this word had connotations of dishonour. Many of my counselling clients had other connotations of giving up control; being possessed; being taken over, and losing ones power. Yet, surrender really means allowing our Higher Self to take over. The true act of SURRENDER means surrendering our ego, surrendering to our own power, which is the SOURCE of All. We can really only surrender to our own power anyway, and it performs better than our ego self, (who thinks it's in control), can ever do. So then, what does surrender really mean?

For this answer, I remembered one of my favourite verses from 1 Corinthians 13, which spoke of : FAITH, HOPE, and CHARITY. On carefully looking at these three words, I discovered how language had changed since they were originally written.

FAITH:

Faith means a deep belief, without any concrete proof. Faith is vital at the beginning of any endeavour. For example, would you have bothered to read this book if you didn't think you would gain something from it, perhaps an inspiration, or some knowledge, or even entertainment. We started in faith, and every new venture begins with FAITH. Even the simple action of walking requires FAITH. We push ourselves forward and momentarily lose our balance, and have FAITH that the other leg we move out will support us. The first step towards Self-Realisation is achieved through Faith. It is the basis of Christianity.

It reminds me of a wonderful story called 'Footprints in the Sand', by an unknown author:

One night a man had a dream. He dreamed he was walking along the beach with God. Across the sky flashed scenes from his life. For each scene, he noticed two sets of footprints in the sand; one belonged to him, and the other to God.

When the last scene of his life flashed before him, he looked back at the footprints in the sand. He noticed that many times

76

along the path of his life there was only one set of footprints. He also noticed that it happened at the very lowest and saddest times in his life. This really bothered him and he questioned God about it.

"Lord, you said that once I decided to follow you, you'd walk with me all the way. But I have noticed that during the most troublesome times in my life there is only one set of footprints. I don't understand why when I needed you most you would leave me."

God replied, "My precious, precious child, I love you and I would never leave you. During your times of trial and suffering, when you see only one set of footprints in the sand, - IT WAS THEN THAT I CARRIED YOU."

Faith is understanding that we live in an Abundant and loving Universe which is here for our highest GOOD.

HOPE:
The ancient meaning of hope really meant TRUST, which is another way of saying acceptance. The modern meaning of hope is hoping for something that we have no control over. In this context Hope is based upon fear that we may not get what we want after all. TRUST on the other hand knows it will receive. Such a being has Faith and knows all its wants and needs will be met. There is no element of fear. Hope implies fear, and doubt that we will receive. Trust affirms we will receive all that we seek.

A student of Truth on the path need not hope for enlightenment anymore than a healthy apple tree need hope for fruit. It knows it is forthcoming automatically. The limitation of hope can be best typified by the following story:

An explorer, while moving through unchartered jungle, fell into a very deep, narrow, and vertical cave. He was saved from injury by landing in an underground stream at the bottom, the water being waist deep. Searching around in the dim light, looking for a way out, he found to his relief, a number of vines hanging down from the top of the cave. He grabbed the strongest one, but before he had reached halfway up, the vine gave way, dropping him back into the stream. He tried the next vine, which also collapsed. Then the next with the same results. With one remaining vine left, he looked fearfully at his last hope. If this should fail, he would be doomed. Perhaps if he should wait for a while, comforting himself with the hope that the last remaining vine would save him, he thought. No, better to face the outcome, one way or another. With hands trembling with fear, he reached up and began pulling himself carefully upward. A quarter of the way up, it also collapsed, and down he fell. His spirits were utterly crushed as a wave of horror overcame him. All hope was gone, and he would surely die. He found a rock at the bottom of the stream and sat down on it in the water to await his eventual death. After a time sitting there, he had a strange sense of calmness that many condemned people tend to experience. Within that stillness he became aware of the water he was sitting in, as it flowed passed him. Slowly, an idea began to filter into his mind. Bending down into the water, he picked up the rock he had been sitting on, and with several other large rocks he plugged the hole where the water flowed out. Soon, the cave began to fill with water, and as it rose, he rose with it, until, eventually he rose to the top and managed to escape.

Every outcome is perfect when we have the courage to face and abandon our false hopes. Trust; it is safe to Trust.

CHARITY:

The ancient meaning of CHARITY was unconditional Love. The modern version of charity has a totally different meaning from the original. For example, a millionaire has a totally different meaning of charity to a person living on the bread line.

The enlightened soul, Paul, who wrote the words in his letter to the Christians at Corinth, meant: to love with ones whole being without expecting anything in return. How many of us can really love like that. Such a love comes from a purity of consciousness that is free of addictions, fears, and suppressions.

"If I speak with the eloquence of men and of angels, but have no love, I become no more than the blaring brass or crashing cymbal.

If I have the gift of foretelling the future and hold in my mind not only all human knowledge but the very secrets of God, and if I also have that absolute faith which can move mountains, but have no love, I amount to nothing. If I dispose of all that I possess, yet, even if I give my own body to be burned, but have no love, I achieve precisely nothing.

This love of which I speak is patient and kind. It is not possessive: it is neither anxious to impress nor does it cherish inflated ideas of its own importance.

Love has good manners and does not pursue selfish advantage. It is not touchy. It does not keep account of wrongs or gloat over the wickedness of other people, for it rejoices in the truth.

Love knows no limit to its endurance, no end to its trust, it can outlast anything.

In life there are three great lasting qualities - Faith, Trust and Love. But the greatest of them is Love." Corinthians 13.

Integration of the three functions, Intellect, Emotions, and Physical is realised through Faith, Trust, and Love and to achieve this state of awareness, we surrender our petty egos, and attachment to thoughts, emotional expectations, and physical demands that tell us we need in order to be happy. The way of ENLIGHTENMENT is the path of SURRENDER, the way of NON-STRIVING.

It is Great to have Faith; it is Powerful to Trust, it is Wonderful to Love; it is Safe to Surrender.

We do live in a loving and supportive Universe. We may not experience it at this stage, yet we can change our reality to experience it, if we really want to. And how do we do that? Just relax, have fun and all will be well.

GEMS ALONG THE WAY

* Surrender is the path of Non-Striving.
* Faith is the cornerstone of all achievement.
* Give up the need for 'hope'.
* Faith, Trust, and Love are the elements to 'Self-Realisation.
* Unconditional Love is the greatest of the three.

CHAPTER NINE

PERFECTION
THE FIFTH COMPONENT

'What ever happens is perfect' is like a non-statement, and yet, it encompasses the other four Components in it's importance.

The dictionary describes the word 'perfection' as completion, full development; perfect specimen or manifestation. I would describe it as Integration, leading to Bliss Awareness.

Perfection is known through the experience of Bliss Awareness and is a state of non-illusion: i.e. being clear of limiting beliefs and thoughts that prevent our natural flow of love, aliveness, and creative self-expression. It is a state of self-Realisation - of realising the True Self within. That is all.

'Self Realisation' means being at home with ourselves, loving our own company, and feeling at peace within ourselves. This is authentic Bliss.

To begin to understand the true meaning of Bliss, it may be necessary to first know what it is not.

Bliss is not exterior activity and excitement, or pleasant emotions. Pleasures of the exterior world such as power, possessions, security, affection from others, sex, fine food, gratifying physical feelings, may merely be a distraction from inner unhappiness. There is nothing wrong with any exterior attractions, and they do draw out a small portion of our true inner Bliss.

Bliss has no form; it cannot be weighed, measured, seen, felt, tasted, heard or smelt. It cannot be fitted into a frame work of demands or expectations. We may insist that people and things satisfy our demands and as long as they do, we are reasonably content. But when they fail to comply, we feel unhappy. So then, what is Bliss? The answer is simple...

Bliss is consciously experiencing our Perfection, and a state of inner freedom. It is freedom from all that is false, and therefore limited. It is not the absence of so-called negative emotions but rather a freedom from being controlled by such emotions that make us feel inadequate, alienated, and separate. It is not in having desire, but rather a freedom from our painful addictions that crave for people, things and activities, addictions that insist we need in order for us to be happy. It is not an absence of fear, but rather a freedom from being controlled by it.

Bliss is not always logical, and it has a timeless innocence about it.

St. Francis of Assisi would probably be commited to an asylum if he lived today. Talking to trees, saying, "Sister, how are you today?" To the almond tree he would say, "Sing to me of God dear brother", and he heard the song that the almond tree sang! What a crazy man. He spoke to the river and to the fish, claiming that they responded to him. He was seen talking to rocks and birds. What further proof do we need that he was mad. But did he care? His capacity to hear the almond tree sing, and a heart that can feel brothers and sisters in trees, the heart that can talk to rocks and birds, the heart that sees God everywhere, all around, in every form. If this be madness, then I request my fill of such a heart. Such a heart is of pure love which reveals that mystery deep within us. But for the logical mind, of course, this is all nonsense.

Such is the nature of Bliss, for it is an experience which cannot be explained in words any more than trying to explain the experience of seeing the colour blue to a person born blind. No book or teacher can tell us what Bliss really is. We can only be guided to experience it for ourselves. Only then will we truly understand.

We begin to understand by realising that feelings of pleasure are not the same thing as Bliss. Pleasure is related to attractions outside ourselves, which act to satisfy us, at best, temporarily. Bliss is the experience from within.

The majority of people, spend all their time avoiding pain by striving to attain happiness. Because we have lost touch with our Inner Wisdom, we try to escape pain and pursue pleasure, mistaking it for Bliss. The attainment of Bliss is universally the same for every person who achieves it, whereas pleasure is different and changeable for each person. In other words, what satisfies one does not necessarily satisfy another. And each is never satisfied with only one object of pleasure. We need to be stimulated continuously with a stream of countless entertainments, lest we become bored with ourselves. There is a restlessness that demands satisfaction, and so we constantly fall into pain, even though we work very hard to avoid it by adopting behaviours we think will free us from our agony. Yet, the insatiable craving follows whereever we go. This shows the false nature of pleasure. Truth is unchangeable and constant, whereas the fleeting, false nature of pleasure depends on external change and stimuli to be maintained.

There is no suggestion that we stop enjoying life and the exterior attractions. In fact the opposite becomes true. Once we become free from our craving for stimulation and the fleeting pleasures, we can actually enjoy them more, because we are free from the fear that our pleasures may be taken away. So we can enjoy them while they last and enjoy ourselves when they are gone.

These ideas emphasize the need for more awareness and for realising the truth of who we really are, - a Divine Spiritual Being.

To expand awareness, we need to start looking for the perfection in everything, including ourselves. The truth is we are perfect and so is everyone and everything else. In fact, there is nothing bad, evil, horrible or even unpleasant in the universe. It is only our belief in evil, and our limited perception of our world that keeps us from seeing the Perfection.

THE GARDEN OF EDEN:
Perfection is symbolized in the Bible when it talks about the Garden of Eden. The Garden of Eden is man's original conscious state of communion with the Absolute, when we were one with all Consciousness. As it is written, God commanded Adam (humanity) to eat fully from the tree of life and enjoy total Abundance. To eat is to experience the outer physical world as well as our Inner Source, and Life and Perfection is our true

Source. God also warned against eating from the Tree of the Knowledge of Good and Evil (duality), though it was enjoyable to look upon. The serpent is the symbol for the part of our intelligence, for example, logic, that decided it wanted part of the universe just for itself. And so Adam ate from the Tree of Knowledge of Good and Evil and created the first ego which in turn created the first dualistic thinking such as good versus evil, discrimination and value judgements, and began to acknowledge THIS as his source. That is, he thought that he could be good and bad, and this separated humanity from it's true Source, God, who is beyond such limitations. The One became the many and we are all part of that flow.

Society is proud (vanity) of its intelligence and ability to discriminate between good and bad - the ability to understand what is right and what is wrong. Opinions and value-judgements are so important to us and yet, it is these very things that we need to let go of in order to experience our Source. We need to see beyond such limitations. Vanity, characterised by his ability to judge, was Satan's downfall, and his sin was wanting to be God, but his pride stopped him from seeing he already was! Satan represents the ignorance and arrogance of people, and the thinking that we will never reach perfection. This separates us from our Source, and results in pain and suffering. We know what hell is like; we are there when we believe we are unloved and that our pain and limitation will last forever. Once we began believing ourselves to be less than God, suffering be came possible, and this is known as the original sin. All ignorance is based on original sin, and original sin is the only sin that exists. It was born when we stopped believing in our divinity. At birth we commit original sin by buying into the ideas of helplessness and fear, which has been described as birth trauma.

The word "sin" in its ancient meaning was to miss the mark that one was aiming for, but today's meaning carries sinister connotations of "evil". The word evil is the word 'live' spelt backwards. The only evil that exists is when we try to live life back to front, by missing the mark of understanding who we really are . Every other thought to do with evil and sin stems from man-made rules designed to manipulate people into behaving in a particular way and following a particular creed. So to sin is to deny our own perfection and the perfection of everyone else. The only evil that exists is created by judging something as wrong, by hating it, denying or ignoring it, and holding a belief that something is bad, wrong, evil or even unpleasant. Everything created comes from truth, so how can anything be bad?

If the devil himself walks in, love him and he will turn into God, the God he always was. The concept of sin is supported by people who have yet to understand their own inner conflicts. In its modern connotation, it is an error to call anyone a sinner. It is a libel on human nature. Sin does not exist, only error, and the only error there is, is to think that we are limited and are sinners.

We all act strangely at times, unloving and angry, and it is because we have for gotten who we really are, forgotten that we are born with the essence of the Divine within us.

In reality, judgements don't exist except in the mind of the person experiencing them. In other words, there is no such thing as good, any more than there is any such thing as bad. Even the word 'Perfection' is just another value-judgement. Saying that something is perfect or imperfect, or even more or less desirable, is simply not true.

So, what is Perfection? Perfection is a state of being, of pure existence. It just IS! It is only the ego that insists that such values as good or bad exist. Of course, by doing certain things we can add to our satisfaction and good health. Other things can be created to work against us. With greater awareness we can see what is counter-productive and what is effective, for no self-aware person hurts themselves through unaware actions.

And even this is not entirely true. Whenever we do something which has an unproductive outcome, like creating a situation where others or ourselves may feel hurt, life gets us in touch with any falseness operating within us through our feelings. There is no judgement, but simply what is TRUE and what is FALSE. No judgement - just awareness. With awareness, everything works, there is total satisfaction in every action and event, and we can see that everything is for our highest good. Everyone is in the right place, doing the right thing, at the right time. "So why try to push against the flow of the river"?

The next question that arises from this is: if everything is perfect, then our limitations and negativity must also be perfect, is that right?

Indeed, Yes, if they existed. Remember, only truth is real, falseness doesn't exist. Limitation doesn't exist. It is only our belief in falseness which makes it appear real to us. A so-called something that isn't real cannot be perfect nor imperfect, because it is nothing. Limitation is the same: to try to put a value judgement on something that doesn't exist is simply ridiculous, yet we do it everyday. We see someone stealing, and we say that person is wrong to do that. All we have done is to perpetuate the thief's made-wrong. Whatever we concentrate our thoughts on, or put our energy to anything, we give the action more power and

87

create more of it. That is why introducing tougher laws to suppress crime never works. In fact it has the opposite effect. Suppressing something may put it out of the way for a while, but eventually it must resurface to bother us. What happens when you sweep a dead rat under the mat? After a few days it begins to smell. Greater awareness, Compassion and Understanding are the only solutions to curbing the rising crime figures. The increasing number of committed crimes is telling us to be more aware, compassionate, and understanding. Yet, in our 'waking unconsciousness' we react by increasing punishments, and wonder why the crime figures continue to soar.

Value-judgements are only concepts of thought and are based upon our beliefs. For example, a person may celebrate when the house of an enemy burns down, but the enemy is grief stricken! Same action, but two entirely different viewpoints. A belief in duality always leads to suffering, because it is opposed to one-ness. One-ness is perfection and Reality; duality is a belief in opposites and separation. And such a belief is also perfect.

Society is quick to judge when things appear to go wrong, and find someone to blame as a form of solution. We see a friend being victimized by someone else, and rather than see how our friend may be attracting such treatment to themselves through unconscious self-contempt, we are quick to rescue them and prevent their healing and self-discovery.

We judge the actions of one group against another as being an injustice, and take up the cry of protest. Rather than see the deeper need for healing and integration of two differing ideas, we add more energy to the polarization and separateness.

My own teacher, Michael Freedman once said something that had a profound effect on my thinking in understanding the process of Integration.

"When you see two opposing truths, by looking at the high point in between, and by going high enough, you will eventually see how they are both the same."

We see one nation invade another, and rush to their defense without seeing the metaphysical causes of such actions. And everytime we react without true awareness, an awareness which comes from compassion and understanding, we prevent ourselves from seeing the perfection of the event.

Thus we are a world that stumbles from one disaster (learning process) to the next, each time adding more energy to perpetuate the original 'made wrong' perception, through the polarization of dualistic thinking. Dualism is a belief in two supreme and opposing powers in the world, such as good verses evil; each in perpetual conflict. Some even believe that two such forces are necessary to maintain balance in the world. Balance, harmony and perfection just are, and are not supported by the need for violent confrontation between two opposing forces. Such a belief may spring from a fear of evil.

BELIEF IN EVIL IS ONLY UNRESOLVED FEAR:

Perfection is easier to understand when we realise that ego (conditioning) is based on fear. All superstition, all evil, all things we call bad or wrong are simply a reflection of the unresolved fears of the hurt and frightened child we all have bottled up inside.

Many people are raised on such a dualistic belief system.

Watch an hour of television or any movie and there is always the good guy against the bad guy. The bad guy eventually loses of course and the good guy becomes the hero. The good guy wins through actions that are often as violent as those of his opponent, which sets up in the minds of people that violence is an effective and an appropriate form of behaviour.

Good must triumph over evil, is a popular notion and appears in many exoteric religions and philosophies.

*Jehoshuwah Ben-Miriam (Jesus) was an esoteric teacher who taught that the Kingdom of God was within every person, and that "perfect love casts out fear." Gandhi once said that the only devils that exist are those who run around in the hearts of men. Yet, the fear of God has been a popular notion for a long time. This is a belief in punishment and reward which is a hangover from an upbringing in which we experience manipulation. This type of upbringing creates fear, which leads to a belief in good and evil. Exoteric religion (the popular doctrines) teaches that evil is real in order to keep their flock believing in a certain direction, and what better way than teaching of a punishing God (an extention of parental disapproval). "Sin will bring death and damnation", and to a person committed to such an idea, evil appears to be a very real entity, and they experience it through their fear. Superstition is built on fear. But, when a person truly examines their feelings through Higher awareness, the fears begin to dissolve. When the fears are gone, all that is left is perfect love. This understanding makes us realise that the universe is love and nothing but love.

*Jehoshuwah Ben-Miriam was the real name of Jesus. Jesus is a Greek name. Jehoshuwah was changed to Jesus when the Bible was translated into Greek.

That all is God and nothing but God. Everything else we experience that is not love is the result of learnt habits of early childhood conditioning. It seems that children are taught fear from the time they are born (birth trauma), which is reinforced by well-meaning but mis-directed adults who manipulate their children into behaving through ploys of punishment and reward. Thus fear becomes a controlling factor in most peoples lives. So it is not surprising that the idea of a devil and evil became popular so long ago and remains in the minds of many people today.

I quote from 'YOUR RIGHT TO RICHES':

"It's interesting that spiritual groups give 'lip' service to the belief that God is Omni-present, that He or She is everywhere and in the same breath speak of evil and lack as a reality. Now you can't have it both ways. Either God is everywhere and is everything, which means evil cannot exist, because if it did then a part of God would also be evil; or God is not Omni-present which means God is separate from humankind.

There is nothing in the universe but Consciousness (Love). All Consciousness is Divine Substance which is God. Material things are just Consciousness made into form. Therefore, everything in creation is perfect, because it is God. The idea that God would create something that wasn't perfect is an admission of a lack of faith. Being materialistic is not a sign of being unspiritual, unless material things are worshiped in place of God. Devotion to material things is putting God (and our power) outside ourselves. But recognizing the God within, allows us to more clearly see the God without, in the form of material things . The clearer we become in ourselves, the more we will realise that all creation is part of the One Universal Consciousness".

As we give up our fears, we will find that all our beliefs about anything outside ourselves having the ability to harm us, also leaves us. The truth is that nothing outside of us can hurt, or have any hold over us what-so-ever. So called competitors in business are not competitors in reality. Believing them to be so is based upon the fear that they can take business away from us or hurt us in some way. But the fear is in us, and not the competitor, so where does the problem lie? It is like bumping our foot on a rock and saying the pain is in the rock. Yet, most people see outside events, people and circumstances as the cause of their lives not working. It is the hurt child inside crying out for love, understanding, and recognition. While they continue to blame others, the hurt child inside remains trapped and unrecognised. Once the 'victim' child is discovered and healed through the five components, there is no-one, no organisation, no government, no set of circumstances that can hold us down and control, or prevent us from growing unless we say they can. It was when we gave our power away through our fear, we gave up experiencing our Divinity.

There are many individuals and groups involved in what we might perceive as evil; such as terrorism, military aggression, torture, dishonest business take-overs , murder, rape, extortion and crime. Most of these people believe they are doing the right thing and don't see themselves as evil doers. Did the priests of the inquisition see themselves as bad? On the contrary, as they tortured and painfully executed the heretics in the name of God, they saw themselves as saints. The petty thief does not see him or herself as wrong, but simply believe the world owes them something and the act of taking something from someone else is in their eyes, perfectly alright. And within their consciousness they are right, because we create our own reality. And who are we to judge their actions. When we sit in judgement of others, we may in our arrogance believe we know better than they, and so dish out the rewards or punishments, the same way as society has always done. It is not surprising that the world is still in the grip of war, famine and disease in spite of this so-called 'enlightened age'. Judgements and comparisons are the work of the ego, and serve only to keep us chained to a low level of awareness.

When individuals and society gives up this need to judge and see only the perfection in everything, they will attract to themselves only truth and beauty. For everything is perfect. Humans are perfect. Some of their actions may appear incorrect and pain producing. This is because they are still committed to the belief in the duality of good and bad. The universe responds not with punishment, but as a loving and generous universe teaching humans all the time that they are judging Perfection as wrong. The stronger they try to prove that things are wrong, the more Life responds with a message of love and teachings which they may interpret as disaster, pain and suffering.

But how can we accept as being perfect those who commit murder and rape and acts of terrorism against innocent victims?

First of all, at a deepest Spiritual level of the True Self, we are totally innocent, because the Divine part of us is incorruptible. So, when discussing earthly events, we are discussing ego, and the Law of Cause and Effect. At this earthly level we gave up our innocence when we took on duality and ego, and have believed ourselves to be guilty ever since.

GUILT IS SELF-HATE:

People who see their own actions as bad, and most of us at times have some regrets, are motivated by a seething self contempt, and this is ultimately self destructive. They are as much victims of society as the people they hurt. They have a strong death urge which is mostly unconscious, and they are almost powerless against the ego. They are so destructively conditioned by the ego that they need much love and care. To punish them sets up a pattern within any society to create even more victims. Punishing such people makes them feel guilty, and guilt has a strong tendency to perpetuate the negative behaviour through self punishment. When a person feels regret over some aspect of their lives, this is a form of self-hate. They may change their behaviour temporarily, but subconsciously the self-rejection reinforces the belief that they are bad and need punishing.

There is only love and joy. This is perfection. All else is just human games, and is illusion. People are not bad or wrong. They are just different and that's perfect.

GEMS ALONG THE WAY:

* BLISS IS A STATE OF NON-ILLUSION
* YOU ARE IN A STATE OF TOTAL BLISS WHETHER YOU ARE AWARE OF IT   OR NOT
* THE GLORIOUS PRESENT MOMENT IS THE ONLY REALITY
* BELIEF IN EVIL IS ONLY UNRESOLVED FEAR
* JUDGEMENT and COMPARISONS CAUSE UNHAPPINESS
* EVIL IS MISSING THE MARK AND LIVING LIFE BACK TO FRONT

CHAPTER TEN

SELF RESPONSIBILITY

It has often been asked if the 'everything is perfect' philosophy, could act as a kind of cop-out, or an excuse to get what we want at others expense, or an excuse to hurt others and avoid responsibility for one's actions. A fair question!

This philosophy very much respects the existence of the natural laws of the Universe, which in broad terms as they relate here are, 'Cause and Effect'. If I were to kill someone, I have then created a cause which will create an effect that will come back to me. For every action there is a reaction. Whatever we put out, must come back to us. 'As you sow, so shall you reap'. However, the higher realms of consciousness have fewer laws governing them. The higher we go, the fewer laws govern us until eventually, we become the law. A master is someone who has mastered all the Universal laws and probably even the highest law, the law of Life Itself.

As a person expands their awareness, they discover the truth that states: 'We create our own reality'! This is a fundamental truth and is demonstrated in every area of our lives. If you pass a thought through your mind enough times, it begins to be accepted as a belief. Beliefs begin to crystalise into experience and experience manifests into reality. So what we believe in becomes our reality. Adolf Hitler once said "If you tell a lie enough times you begin to believe it yourself". We do create all our experiences completely. But in creating this reality, we also created other people in it to have varying degrees of influence upon us, as we have upon them. No one has created a reality of total isolation from the human race by virtue of being born to a mother, someone to share in those important first few years of our lives.

But, back to the question: The philosophy, 'we create our own reality', can be greatly misused. For example, it could be said that since you create your own reality, I can do anything against you, and you must not react with anger or accusations at my actions, because you created me to hurt you in this way. I had no influence on you; you had influence only on yourself. This means I don't have to listen when you say my behaviour is affecting or hurting you. As it's not part of my reality, I don't have to change my behaviour.

This appears all very well intellectually, but avoids the responsibility of living and closely sharing in the reality of other people. It may keep us comfortable in our comfort zone, but also isolated and separate from the closeness and love of others. Rather than teach self-responsibility and non-attachment, it teaches indifference and dissociation.

By living with such a rigid philosophy, we really have a problem when others begin to mistreat us. As I create my own reality, I am denied the response of feeling angry. I must not feel angry because I created it all and so suppress such feelings.

In truth, we have all created our own reality, but it is a

reality where we have influence on others and they have an influence on us.

In a limited level of awareness, it appears that other people and situations create reality for us, and that we are directed by outside agencies. As we awaken a little, we realise that we are ultimately creating it all. With a little more awakening, we begin to understand the relationship and responsibility of the influence others have on us and we have on them. When we pretend that we are totally isolated from the influence of others, or deny we have influence on them, we are likely to avoid having close relationships and understanding with them, and any relationship that does exist will be distant and lacking compassion. But, by accepting that yes we do create our own reality, and yes we do have a strong influence on others as they have on us, only then will we become free within ourselves. We will be free because we will be able to see our ego reacting from the negative influence from others and the defenses we erect that feed into that influence. With this understanding, we are always able to choose how we respond to other people's actions and how we treat them in return, ever aware of the relationship we have with others and the relationship we have with the great law of 'Creating our own reality'.

Self Responsibility means our choice of 'response' to any situation. Our ability to respond means responding to ourselves as the creator of all thoughts, feelings and actions. As the thinker, feeler and actor, we are not our thoughts, emotions and actions, rather the creator of such phenonema.

The old conditioning that I personally grew up with was that it was acceptable in the eyes of society for a man to express his anger, but not O.K. for a woman. Yet, woman could express fear, but not men. An angry man was expressing his natural assertiveness, but if a woman expressed anger, it was regarded as 'unlady like'. It was regarded as natural for a woman to express fear, but for a man to express his fear, he would be regarded as a whimp, a coward etc.

In the new 'Personal Growth' movement, the roles have somehow been reversed. It is now fashionable for men to express their fear, (an emotion that has been suppressed for so long). But they must not express their anger in some circles, for if they do they are regarded as being dominantly aggressive. In some new age movements for men to even be assertive runs the risk of being accused of being aggressively chauvanistic.

Women are now being encouraged to express their anger and it is often interpreted as expressing their assertive rights, particularly when men are involved. But, they must not show fear, for to do so carries the accusation of being passive, a victim and pathetic. All this is just another version of stereo-typing behaviour in reverse.

FATE AND CREATING YOUR OWN REALITY:
The fatalistic philosophy states that our lives are already mapped out and decided upon long before we even arrived here. Thus we have no control over life, and live it out being able to influence only small changes along the way. This appears a total contradiction to creating your own reality. Yet, in higher understanding, both view points are in fact saying the same thing. The fatalist understands their own limitation and power-lessness to change anything major at their present level of development. This is valuable knowledge in recognising the power of the ego, and the importance of surrendering to Perfection. Before we were born, we decided in advance the type of life

that was necessary for us to have in order to learn certain things. Our mission in life is to find knowledge, joy, and fulfillment. These are achieved through the power of love. And the most important thing to learn is to receive and to give love. Our evolvement is controlled by the level of consciousness we have developed so far. Thus, in preparing for a new life, where we are born, who we are born through, and the type of people who will be around us during each stage, will depend upon the level of consciousness we begin with. This is saying: we chose our parents, we chose our body, our mind, our intellect, personality, the culture we were born into, and above all, the patterns of limitations, fears, and conditioning. We created all this well in advance for the purpose of creating a particular reality, in order to disprove the illusion of suffering. We chose certain parents and situations that would put us into life at exactly the same level of our consciousnesswe have evolved to. We can only choose and experience freedom at the level of consciousness we have developed. Many of us have to experience a certain amount of suffering and struggle until we finally begin to awaken and see the games the ego puts us through. Then our consciousness begins to expand. The fatalist understands this and recognizes the futility of trying to use effort and willpower to change it. It is a waste of time and virtually impossible to achieve change of any significance through effort and will power.

There is a way to bring about change and that is through the power of the breath and through impartial observation. This is done by simply being aware of our struggle and resistance (second Component), without demanding that it all change, (Third component). It is the ego, uncomfortable with the present moment, that insists changes are necessary. The second Component of Breath Integration is the key to developing Higher Consciousness through being aware. It is through greater awareness that we can see how controlled we are by the ego, and how much energy and time we waste by trying to avoid the present moment and make changes through effort and trying. The Fifth Component, 'Everything is Perfect', enables us to release the strain of trying to make something happen, and allow it to happen when its ready. There is no race or hurry. We have all of eternity to reach Self Realisation, so there is time to smell the flowers along the way. With this understanding, we begin to manifest Higher Consciousness and Self Responsibility.

Self Responsibility is not always a comfortable principle to accept, because it requires us to give up all our defense mechanisms, our excuses and blaming others as to why our life isn't working. Self Responsibility can only happen once the hurt child within is healed. Until that happens we will find it easier to blame others - "she hurt my feelings", - "he embarrassed me", and when we run out of people or things to blame, we can always blame the government.

A metaphysical Law states that the person who experiences an effect is the person who originally created the cause. If we arrive home to find it burnt to the ground by an arsonist, it has nothing to do with him. As far as we are concerned, we created the situation and the arsonist was simply the instrument for a negative unconscious wish to punish ourselves. The arsonist is responsible for his own experience, and his experience combines with ours to fulfill an unconscious negative desire. Often, negative experiences that happen now are the results of negative thinking years previous, and the Creative mind has taken this long to manifest them.

All accidents, disease and strife are created by the people

who experience them.   In truth there is no such thing as accidents. The universe is too lawful for that. At the base level of existence, all is very mechanical and rigidly controlled by strict laws. But, as developing and evolving creative beings, throught the power of Higher Consciousness, we become less mechanical, less controlled, and more aware, more in charge of ourselves and our environment.

All these ideas can appear quite radical when first exposed to them. I recall some years ago when these concepts were less known, I was giving a public lecture in Auckland on this subject. I had been running a series of lectures on metaphysics, spread over ten weeks, with one lecture per week. There were about fifty people attending on a regular basis. The subject of Self Responsibility and creating your own reality came up on the seventh lecture, and I really gave it to them. I pulled no punches in my enthusiasm. The following week, fourteen people turned up! My closest friends pointed out to me that perhaps I could have been a little more gentle in putting the ideas across. Others suggested that perhaps the majority of people are still not willing to accept that ultimately we are all responsible for everything that happens to us.

Yet, on the surface, this all appears to be devoid of compassion. How does one brush off the plight of the starving millions in the world, the sexualy abused child, the rape victim by saying they chose their situation? A fair comment I think.

When we only look at surface things, that is what we see. When we look only at a part of life, we only see that part and may conclude that it is the whole. When you look at one experience in your life in relation to all Universal life, time, and space, and consider all you have experienced and will experience, the drama of one experience is tiny in comparison. It is all consuming when we limit our viewpoint and only see the limitation. It is allowing one small ego to control our whole being, because it is only the ego we can see.

Every one of us, those in hospitals, prisons, countries in turmoil, all the victims of the world, are all playing out the fulfillment of a self-destructive goal we put in motion when at some point, we judged perfection as wrong. The patterns in our lives remain the same as long as we continue to reinforce them with more ' made wrongs'. If we focus only on all that is wrong with life, that is exactly what we will find.

Yet on the positive side, we can change all this in a minute. The beauty of this philosophy is that we discover we can begin to create the reality we want. We can put ourselves back in the driver's seat of our own lives and take charge of it. This begins to happen when we master the principle of Self Responsibility.

Yet, who is really responsible for what happens? For example, who is responsible for the execution by firing squad of a prisoner?
The person who gives the order, or the person who pulls the trigger?

Think about that for a few minutes. You may find an interesting answer at the end of this chapter.

Self Responsibility does not mean blaming ourselves and going off on a guilt trip. This is merely shifting the desire to punish others, to punishing ourselves. WE ARE RESPONSIBLE BUT NEVER GUILTY. Guilt comes from fear, and the desire to beat ourselves up.

When people first begin to understand these principles, often they can't wait to convert the world to this wonderful new understanding. They might say to people who have issues, or who wanted to clear misunderstandings with them, or who just want to share some of their feelings and difficulties they are having, "Well, that's your problem mate. Why are you attracting this into your life?". This will keep people at a distance and sometimes create a lot of resentment in the other person. It can also reinforce the other persons own self-rejection and guilt in being confront in such a judgemental way. Perhaps we may be trying to teach people things that we have no right to teach. I sometimes hear new comers to 'new Age' thinking, handing out advice to people who are experiencing a lot of drama in their lives, advice that is not invited. It is not very compassionate to tell a woman who has just been raped that she attracted that to herself. It is not compassionate to inform an accident victim that he did it to himself. It may be true that they did do it to themselves, but they don't want to hear such things when they are going through the pain. They won't be receptive to it anyway. What they need is love and understanding. We act responsibly when we give them what they need.

Self Responsibility is not divorcing oneself from how we treat other people and their response back to us, but rather in being sensitive in our response to them. Certainly, we do not cause other people to be happy or unhappy, yet, we have a responsibility as to how we relate to them. If I am insensitive to someones feelings about death just after they have buried a loved one, by making jokes about funerals, I may attract someones anger. If I spread false rumours or half truths about a certain person, I can expect a somewhat negative reaction.

While operating at a limited level of awareness we are very

mechanical and very much controlled by the influences acting upon us from our environment, other people, and mostly by our personal laws, (ego). We seek to satisfy our creature comforts and needs, ever forgetful that we are much more than that. As we begin to awaken even a little, our thinking expands to higher thoughts of the reality of Perfection, Compassion and Understanding. We begin to feel our emotions, which can be uncomfortable while we are still locked into judging. We begin to feel our physical body and the disharmony within it. All this puts us in touch with the importance of Integrating the intellect, emotions, and physical body. This encourages us to start to take care of ourselves and assume a new sense of responsibilty for every aspect of our lives.

BALANCE:

There are two main types of people in the world; doers and followers. Doers, are often people who are strivers, people who are driven to great achievements. Many of these people lack trust in a generous Universe, thinking they have to do it all themselves. I know this, being a compulsive, high achiever myself. We need to learn to develop more Faith and Trust that Life stands ready to serve and help us. The last three Components, Total Acceptance, Total Relaxation, and Whatever Happens is Perfect, were made for us. Yet, these last three Components are not about lying down and expecting the world to provide us with a living, expecting life to do it all for us without any imput from us. They are all about finding Balance and harmony between achievement and surrender. As Awareness develops, the balance between trusting that all we seek will find us, and creatively creating the reality we want, will occur naturally. There is little balance when the extreme fatalistic pessimist allows the negativity to continue by doing nothing. Nor when the compulsive achiever does not accept the present as being perfect and resist it by trying to change things.

A balance is reached when we trust and know all is perfect, and that we can allow life to happen while consciously moving toward the reality we want by visualising and creating it. Thus, we support Life supporting us.

Write down on a piece of paper these questions, and honestly answer them. Spend some time on these and you may discover something very interesting about yourself.

* All the negative ideas I have about responsibility and duty towards myself, others, and situations are.....

* My reasons for not taking responsibility for my own life are...

* What happens to me when I refuse to take responsibility for my thoughts, feelings and actions?...

* What will I gain by taking responsibility for every aspect of my life?...

GEMS ALONG THE WAY:
* Self Responsibility acknowledges the influence we have on others and the influence they have on us.
* We create our own reality based on our beliefs.
* The person who experiences the effect is the person who created the cause.
* Teach only those who are ready for the message of Self Responsibility.
* All are responsible for the execution by firing squad, including the prisoner.

CHAPTER ELEVEN

MANIPULATION AS A DEFENCE

Few subjects have been more written about than that of love and relationships, and yet, misunderstanding and mystery still surround the subject of effectively relating to the people in our lives. This might have something to do with our inability to relate to ourselves. Because of the magnitude of this subject, let us confine our discussion to one important area that prevents us from living in ideal, Loving Relationships with everyone around us.

EMOTIONAL MANIPULATION:

A common form of behaviour is people trying to get what they want by emotionally manipulating others, particularly those who are close to them. The practice of emotional manipulation is like using other people's feelings as a football. We kick it around until they give in to what we want. Manipulation means trying to make others feel bad, wrong, ignorant or guilty. Interestly enough, it is a process that works, but it is dishonest. We know we have been manipulated when someone asks us to do something we don't feel comfortable about, and on our refusal they may respond with:

* *"What about all those times I did such and such for you".* *Implying that we owe them something.*
* *"Oh, well I guess I'll have to do it on my own, me and my bad*

back and all". Subtly telling us we are unkind for not helping.
* *"How come you won't sign this petition? Everyone else in the street has". An implication that we are different and therefore wrong.*
* *"You don't want to buy these valuable encyclopedias? Don't you care for your children's education?" Trying to make us feel as if we are an uncaring parent.*
* *"Why can't I go to the picnic? Nicky's mother is letting her go". As if to say that that Nicky's mother is a better mother for letting her go.*

There are many forms of manipulation and each one implies obligation, through trying to make us feel guilty, inadequate, in the wrong, or bad if we don't comply. It is an attempt by another person to control our behaviour and motivate us in the direction they want us to go.

People use manipulation because they don't know how to get their needs met any other way. It is a defense mechanism, based upon the idea that people are not going to give them what they want if they come right out and ask. This is because many people believe that they don't really deserve to have what they want anyway. But as there is a part of themselves that wants their needs met, they feel a great need to justify and give long explanations as to why they should have something. So, the short-cut is to use a strategy to motivate the other person in such a way that makes them feel bad.

Many people are afraid to tell the truth about their feelings. They think others might be offended or threatened by them expressing what they want in an open and honest way.

People use manipulation on others to the degree they are suseptible to it themselves. In other words, we only use something we think will work, and if we know it works on us, then we have a behaviour that we know works on others. Often it runs in families and you can see daughter using the same form of manipulation that mum or dad used. And probably the same form as the grandparents used. Very soon, the young children start to use it, and where do you think they learnt it from?

The important thing to understand, is that the manipulator needs a victim as much as the victim needs the manipulator. In other words, what would happen if all the victims of the world suddenly vanished? The manipulators wouldn't be able to find anyone to manipulate and the either the behaviour would cease, or they would find other manipulators to become victims. If all the manipulators suddenly disappeared, the victims would create other victims to become manipulators. It's all a game, but in this game, ultimately there are no winners. Even if we get what we want from the other person in this fashion, there is a part of us that has lost some respect for them, which can be traced back to a lack of self respect. In the manipulation game, both sides are victims of perceiving a world that supplies what they need only through others. Because they haven't found themselves and their own ability to be happy within, they seek gratification through others.

Many people have what could be termed as a 'victim' mentality. This is the hurt child within that was mentioned earlier. Such a condition is often accompanied by a low self esteem, and a subconscious belief that they don't deserve anything that is good or perfect. If something really wonderful happens to them like someone falling in love with them, or they win a lot of money, their subconscious 'not good enough' belief comes up and they begin to sabotage the experience. How could this other person love them, and so, in their self-rejection they end the relationship before they think their newly beloved will. This way they get out of the pain of being rejected. This is known as a leaving pattern. Or the person who wins a lot of money will subconsciously find ways of losing it, either through risky investments, or frittering it away on useless trivia.

People who have a low self esteem, and feelings of self hatred [and most people have traces of this] unconsciously teach others to treat them in ways that are unkind. They send out a continuous stream of psychic information that informs others that they are bad, and deserve punishing or ignoring, or stay away. People are treated by others the way they treat themselves. How can we expect anything else? The truth is, we can't. We attract to us a level of consciousness we have within. You can meet someone at a function and within five minutes know the opinion this person has of themselves. You pick up the silent, in-between-the-lines communication the person is emanating which is either self love, or self rejection. You know that you are attracted to people who love and respect themselves, and tend to shy away from those who have a lot of self hate .

Years ago, I meet a beautiful woman who was an ex model. The first month of our relationship was truly magical. I enjoyed being in her company while we were getting to know each other, not so much because of her physical beauty, but because she had such a gentle nature. After a time, I began to find her a little irritating and I couldn't figure out why. Soon I began to snap at her verbally and say things that were unpleasant. I found this strange because it was very uncharacteristic of me. All her previous relationships had ended unhappily and for some reason, the men had been cruel to her. And here I was, just another dominant, aggressive male beginning to make her life unhappy like the others. Our relationship began to decline into manipulating games as we each bought into the other person's power struggles. I was beginning to play her losing game, and the more I unconsciously bought into it, the more I lost as well. In time we discovered the hidden, habitual behaviour patterns we both had that were being activated. My 'stuff' of unconsciously needing someone to dominate me came up. She needed someone to punish her, because she unconsciously believed she was bad. Once we became aware of what we were doing, it became resolved with the help of a lot of Conscious Connected Breathing, and much present moment awareness.

It seems that once we have been with a person for a while and begin to feel a little safer, the protective barriers start to come down, revealing sensitive egos that get easily activated. This has been jokingly described as the finish of the honeymoon period. Relationships change at this point. Either one will start to dominate the more passive personality, or they both try to dominate each other. Manipulation can start to come into play, and unless it is worked through, long term unhappiness can follow.

Manipulating games never work long term if one is seeking a fully harmonious and totally loving relationship. [Oh yes, harmonious and totally loving relationships do exist if you are wondering]. Whenever there is obligation, love flies out the window. Successful relationships are built on trust, respect and freedom. It also means giving up our defenses and being vulnerable and honest with our feelings. It means taking risks with our partner and to say "no", to their manipulating games, which doesn't mean we are saying no to them as a person, or rejecting them. Have the courage to say "no" to the manipulating attempts to control us by our parents, children, spouse, or any close relationships. Say "no" to any attempt which tries to make us do things we would normally choose not to do for ourselves. Break the manipulating cycle and instead, teach others to respect us through the honest sharing of feelings and thoughts. The best way to do that is to be that same way ourselves. Be open to our partner's "no", allowing them to connect with their strength. Give up the need to protect ourselves against the games others feel they need to play against us. This will enable us to see when others are asking for genuine help, and when they are trying to control our behaviour in some way.

When our partner threatens to leave us if we don't change and improve, our defense mechanism will probably drag up all their shortcomings to prove that it is them who needs to change, or we become passive and fall into line and start to 'behave' in order to keep the relationship alive. Perhaps an appropriate response to such a threat without a defense operating could be to agree, that maybe a time a part could be the answer. This would show us if our partner was trying to manipulate us into changing, or that they were being honest about what they wanted. Not buying into a need to defend would bring you both to clarity and inner freedom.

ASSERTIVE LISTENING AND RESPONSE.
Assertive listening is a simple skill that enables you to observe whether the other person is attempting to genuinely help or attempting to exert control over you. With this knowledge we can then respond effectively that is free of protective barriers, and coming from love. Here are some points which highlight the importance of listening carefully to what is said and then responding without using any defense mechanisms:

1. IDENTIFICATION: Observe your fears from the criticisms aimed at making you feel ignorant, anxious or guilty. Realise that only the ego, connected to your poor self esteem can become upset. Even if you have made a mistake, you are not the mistake. Observe your ego playing out it's 'not good enough' games.

2. GIVE UP BEING DEFENSIVE: Don't sound defensive, angry, threatening, sarcastic, blaming, or deny you are in the wrong, or counter attack by pointing out their shortcomings. This builds further Protective Barriers in both you and others. Instead, offer no resistance to other people's attacks or subtle criticisms. Act like a fog bank which doesn't fight back and remains completely unaffected from anything attacking it. If a rock is thrown at a fog, it passes through without any effect. If you throw a rock against a brick wall, the wall acts as a barrier to the rock and on their meeting there is conflict and violence. Being defensive has the same effect. Respond with -
"You may be right."

3. ACCEPT THE POSSIBILITY OF BEING IN ERROR: There is no need to apologise or grovel. But, it can be important to acknowledge our genuine mistakes. Particularly if others have been inconvenienced by our thoughtlessness and they may feel it is important to be heard. Even though we are perfect, because we have an ego, our actions may not always be on target. It is alright for others to see our imperfections and comment or criticise them. In their eyes we may be stupid or look silly and that is their reality. It is a waste of time to defend ourselves or argue with someone else's feelings and perceptions. When we have made an error it can be good to acknowledge with:
"That was rather a foolish thing I did. Is there anything I

can do to compensate for this?"

When others are criticising us and we are comfortable with what we are doing, a good response can be:

"Yes, my actions probably do appear foolish to you." No denying, but simply an acknowledgement of the other person's comments without us having to defend anything. If we don't understand the criticism, ask for more information with:

"I don't understand what it is about me.......that is wrong?" This encourages them to be honest and assertive with you, without the need to use manipulation.

4.   AGREE WITH TRUTH AND IGNORE IMPLICA-TIONS: Listen for the truth people tell you about your behaviour and ignore the implications they attack you with, which are based up on their beliefs of right and wrong. For example if someone said to you: "Your house is a mess...aren't you ashamed?" Perhaps your house is a mess in their eyes, and they are allowed to think that, and you can acknowledge them. Yet you don't have to buy in to the comment on the end "aren't you ashamed?' which is coming from a limiting belief in them. Listen for their truths of observation and ignore the implications they tack on the end, which is designed to manipulate.

EG. "You look terrible in that...don't you have any pride?"

"You may be right. Perhaps I could look better." Or
"You are probably right...."
"I can see that you feel that way..."
"I can see that you think that..."

They say "you are...." Respond with:
"You could be right, I probably am...."

5. FOCUS ON OURSELVES, RATHER THAN ON THEM OR THEIR ATTACK: "What is it about ME doing this, that is wrong?"

Many people instead say this: "What makes YOU think doing this is wrong?", which is really saying - *Who the hell are you to tell me anything?*

By putting the focus on us shows them that we are not attacking them, but, interested in a genuine attempt at conciliation.

"I don't understand. How is my behaviour making you feel bad?" "What is it I'm doing that is making you feel that way?", which is really saying - "Let's look at what I'm doing that could be changed".

6. INVITE FURTHER CRITICISM:

"Is there anything else I'm doing besides....that you don't like?" This exhausts further manipulative attempts and encourages them to be honest with their feelings towards you. This often means the manipulating game stops and they start to assertively describe what is really going on for them, while feeling safe, knowing you are not in a defensive position.

By identifying our fears of not being good enough; dropping all defenses; accepting that we may be in error; agreeing with truth but ignoring those implication s manipulators tack on the end of attacking statements; by focusing on what we may be doing rather than blaming them; and inviting even further criticism; we don't feel the need to protect ourselves, which

115

makes them feel safer. The safer they feel, the less defensive they become. What a beautiful gift we have given ourselves and to them - a chance to lovingly bridge the gap that separates one person from another.

Some people might be inclined to ask, "why even bother to have anything to do with manipulating people?" Well, if you feel the need to stay away from such people, it is probably because they have an effect on you. If this is true that you feel uncomfortable around them, it may be because you have protective barriers up that manipulators bounce off, and that can be very uncomfortable, indeed. But remember, if manipulators affect you this way, consider the fact that there just might be a little manipulator inside you that is reacting, which is why you may feel the need to defend yourself so strongly against them.

Most people it seems have some traces of manipulating behaviour as a defense they learnt while growing up. If you wish not to have any manipulators around you at all, you may be very lonely.

A week before Christmas, 1988, I had brought Kathryn a dress as a present, but when she tried it on, she decided it didn't quite suit her. I agreed to take it back the next day and obtain a refund. I arrived at the shop armed with my assertive techniques, to ask for the refund, and looking forward to the challenge. I started with quietly requesting that as the dress was unsuitable, could I please have my money back, which was greeted with an instant refusal. I applied the 'broken record' stance that works on the idea of repeating what I want until they eventually give in. However, this manageress was as determined as I was in getting her way. So, I suggested a compromise, would she be willing to give me a credit note in exchange for the dress,

116

and Kathryn would spend it in her shop at a later time. The response was that this was not their policy. After about ten minutes of requesting and her denying, during which time the dialogue got progressively more hostile, I made my second mistake, (the first being, that I was being assertive for the wrong reason). I pointed out to the manageress, that as she had no signs up announcing their refund policy, or the lack of it, she was obligated to comply to my wishes. I also threw at her that businesses like the large departmental stores who had integrity wouldn't hesitate to satisfy their customers. This was received with, "Well, why don't you go and shop there instead of hasseling me?" I kept the pressure on , continuing to request a refund, ('broken record') and throwing in, how would she feel in my position; that she had not only a moral obligation but also she was breaking the law in not meeting my demands. In desperation, the poor woman rang the owner of the shop for advice. I insisted on speaking to her to further request my refund. The owner sided with the manageress and hung up in my ear. I believed I was being very reasonable in keeping my 'cool' throughout this ordeal. The manageress began to ignore me and serve other customers. When there were no customers in the shop, I quietly said that I was prepared to wait all day until she gave me the refund, or even the credit note I felt was rightfully mine. She replied angrily "didn't I have things better to do than waste both our times?" and stalked out to the back of the shop. Obviously, this wasn't working. I stood there feeling terrible, suspecting the manageresss was probably feeling much the same. I realised then that I was trying to prove I could win, and was prepared to use all my skills as a motivater, including manipulation to win the day. Was the money for the dress worth this? The next time she came out from the back, I approached her. As she saw me coming she glared at me, and I said, "Look at us. It's Christmas, a season of good will, and here we are at each other's throat. See this dress?" I held it up in both hands and handed it to her, "I want to make a gift of this dress to you, without any money, refund, or even thanks. Please accept it, and I am really sorry that this whole episode has happened between us". She stared back at me disbelieving the total switch in my behaviour. "What!" she answered back.

"I really mean it", I continued, "I feel really stupid for carrying on like this, and so, please take the dress."

"I am astounded", she replied. After what seemed a very long time, both of us staring at each other, her eyes softened, "As you are feeling so different", she said, "Let me put it in the shop window, and when I sell it, I will ring you and give you the full refund".

"No, I want you to have it back for free. No refund is necessary. Establishing peace with you is more important to me right now". I added.

Christmas Eve she rang me and insisted on giving me the money, and we parted as friends.

What this taught me was, in using any techniques, whether they be assertiveness, N.L.P. (Neuro-Linguistic Programming), Transactional Analysis, etc, their effectiveness is more determined by what is in our hearts rather than using them in a manipulative way. I've also seen other people use assertiveness techniques to manipulate others, instead of establishing harmony and trust with others, and this is the same with any skill. We can abuse our knowledge to get what we want at other people's expense. We know we are doing this if we have defenses operating. Let your awareness of what is in your heart be the key!

GEMS ALONG THE WAY:

* Don't identify with feelings of inadequacy - just observe them.
* Give up your protective barriers by not defending, attacking, blaming, denying, or making others wrong.
* Yet, give others permission to make us wrong, for they cannot hurt us.
* Come from love rather than from fear and the need to defend.
* Realising that our True Self does not need defending.

CHAPTER TWELVE

THE MANIPULATING TRIANGLE

Transactional Analysis first presented what they called 'The Drama Triangle', which illustrates the different roles and variety of position-switches that often happen in the course of people relating to one another. I've termed it the 'Manipulating Triangle' and it shows that there are three main roles assumed by characters in the game of life. You can see them clearly displayed in soap operas, and probably in every area of your own life. They are:

1. Oppressor.
2. Rescuer.
3. Victim.

"ALL THE WORLD IS A STAGE":

The oppressor plays the villain, who supposedly preys upon victims, with the intention of controlling and dominating them. The rescuer plays the hero or heroine who enters the game to rescue the victim and defeat the villain. The world generally favours the under-dog, the victim, who plays the part where they are helpless and in need. It's all a game where there are supposedly winners and losers, and is based upon manipulation. Yet, such manipulating games lead to loss of freedom, and unhappiness by all players.

OPPRESSOR
Controller, Blamer -
Has anger,
resentment
and attacks with -
"It's all your fault"
"You are wrong,
selfish
or bad".

Coming from
Fear

RESCUER
I'll make it
better
I know better
I am only trying to
help
I am responsible
for other People's
feelings.

VICTIM
Poor me. I'm helpless or
powerless. I can't do it alone.
I don't know what to do.

1. OPPRESSOR: The Oppressor is someone who has a need to dominate more passive personalities, and be in control. They have a strong critical parent mode, with the sense of duty to punish and reward suboardinants. Such people are controlled by rules and rigid expectations. They have a victim mentality themselves - but are attempting to cover up their fear through their dominating behaviour.

2. RESCUER "The Compulsive Helper." Their prime motive is to get strokes, although this is rarely admitted and they are often quite unaware of such a need. They tend to neglect their own needs, and eventually end up being a victim themselves (burn out). Often they are rejected by those they are trying to rescue because the victim is left dissatisfied as they see the rescuers position as saying - "I'm o.k., you're not o.k. (You're inadequate, I have to do it for You)" Rescuers identify themselves with the victims of the world and have a great need for

approval. They often see themselves as compassionate and understanding, but many times it is 'psuedo' love based upon their own personal need to be recognised and loved, and their attempt to disguise their own inner victim.

3. VICTIM "Poor Me Syndrome." They see themselves as victims of everyone else. They feel they have no control over their lives and are at the mercy of everything and everyone. Often they have a need for security and people to look after them, and so are motivated by fear and a belief in a hostile world.

A person who plays one of these roles, generally has all three buried inside them, just waiting for the right moment to express itself. A person can change roles even within a few minutes, particularly during a conflict situation.

EG: Harry comes through the door and shouts at his wife,
HARRY: "You have forgotten to put out the garbage again. How many times do I have to tell you to remember to do it?" (Oppressor)
MARTHA: looking down trodden, "Oh, dear, I'm sorry. I clean forgot. Please don't shout at me". (victim).
Jenny, Martha's friend from next door interupts with:
JENNY: "Leave Martha alone Harry. I've seen you forget to do a few things around the house from time to time." (rescuer).
Martha changes from the victim stance to the oppressor as she launches an assault of her own.
MARTHA: "Yes, and what about all the times you have forgotten to pick up the dry cleaning. Did you pick it up today?"
Harry's lip drops as he remember's that he forgot (victim).
MARTHA: "Talk about me, you're even more stupid than I am".

No matter if we are an oppressor, rescuer, or victim, we are in those roles because of our defenses and through them we attempt to control other people's behaviour that we see as the cause of our problems. Yet, while we blame others, we stay stuck behind our protective barriers.

All three behaviours unconsciously seek to control or manipulate the other to support their role.

The Oppressor who says - "You are stupid", controls the victim through power and domination games. They often control rescuers in the same way.

The Rescuer who says - "Let me do it for you", controls the victim by making him or her dependant on them. They control the oppressor by becoming an oppressor themselves and turning the oppressor into a victim with subtle criticism, sarcasm, and cynicism.

The Victim who says - "Poor Me" controls the oppressor through attracting the oppressor to play the role in the first place. A passive personality that is coming from fear, doesn't have to wait long for an oppressor to show up and kick them. They further control them through the 'cold silent treatment', or by turning around and pointing out how terrible the oppressor has been. The victim controls the rescuer by playing helpless, and vulnerable, and making the rescuer feel sorry for them.

As stated, they are all victims, and all are coming from fear! Each needs the other to function in their particular role, so they create or attract such persons into their lives to satisfy their unconscious belief in this Manipulating Triangle.

We can identify the oppressor in us and others by observing the following behaviours (defenses):

DEFENSE MECHANISMS OF THE OPPRESSOR:
* Over-reacting to situations with physical or verbal violence.
* Violating other's rights through aggression or manipulation.
* The need to dominate passive personalities.
* Intolerant of defeat and other people's weaknesses.
* Achieving success through power and domination games.
* Expressing opinions, goals or wants in ways which demean, or put down.
* Rebellous or aggressively protest against other oppressors.
* Insensitve to the feelings, ideas, or rights of others.
* A tendancy to be angry or harbour resentments.

We can clearly identify the rescuer in us and others by observing the following defensive behaviours:

DEFENSE MECHANISMS OF THE RESCUER:
* Wanting to take the hurt away from those who are suffering.
* Easily upset by observing the suffering of others.
* Being a placator and wanting everything to be just right.
* Hiding true feelings by being 'so nice'.
* Will do almost anything to win approval.
* Being indirect and finding it impossible to say no and mean it.
* Expressing wants by round-about actions, words and behaviours.
* Being too diplomatic and fearing hurting other people's feelings.
* 'Pussy-footing' around trying to please everyone at once.

A victim is easily identified by the following defensive behaviours:

DEFENSE MECHANISMS OF THE VICTIM:
*   Generally a passive personality as a result of fear.
*   Allowing others to manipulate, control, and dominate them.
*   Letting others make their decisions for them.
*   Sometimes expecting others to second guess their feelings and wants.
*   Needing to justify, and pretending to make excuses to get what they want.
*   Being too afraid to express their feelings.
*   Often denying their own rights.
*   Keeping opinions to oneself-avoiding conflict at all costs.
*   Being frightened of disapproval, but tends to attract a lot of it anyway.
*   Often physically or psychologically ill.
*   Poor self esteem and lack self-confidence, which leads to self put-downs.
*   Fearing what others can do to them.
*   Reacting inappropriately, and apologeticly.
*   Using negative languaging which reinforces their belief in a hostile world.

Everyone wants to get rid of the oppressor. Hitler was probably the number one oppressor of the twentieth century, and was hated by millions. The villain in every novel and film where the hero battles him or her, the 'bad guy', leaves no doubt in everyones mind as to whom is the cause of everyone's problems. Yet, this is approaching the question of who really is the cause of the problem from a limited perspective. Hitler, and all the oppressors of this world, are largely the creation of the victims of the world. If Hitler was not there, someone else would have stepped in and done exactly what he did. He, like every other oppressor is simply an instrument of the victims. If we eliminated the victim mentality everyone carries around with them, the oppressors of the world would suddenly disappear. The victim mentality is also reinforced by the rescuers, who in fact dis-empower the victim, by helping to maintain the victim's helplessness. The rescuers and the oppressors are maintained in their roles by the victims who have an unconscious belief that they need to be punished.

This is not excusing the destructive actions of terrorists or the negative actions of any person playing out the role of oppressor, for they are responsible for their actions. But, society has been trying to eliminate the oppressors since the beginning of time, and continues with tougher laws, (which is playing the same game) and it hasn't worked. There are just as many, if not more oppressors operating than ever before, according to crime figures, etc. Perhaps if people took stock of themselves, and began to let go of the victim, and the hurt and frightened child buried away inside them, the manipulating triangle would cease to operate. Even if we were successful at eliminating all the oppressors, the victims would turn other victims into oppressors, so it is a losing battle. In reality, the oppressor does not take the victims power, the victim gives it. Thus, the victim is the star player in the manipulating triangle, and in fact all three roles are victims in varying degrees.

This whole game can be changed by using the 'Breath Integration Cycle', as described in Chapter Three. This is helped by each player, clearly identifying their particular role, and seeing it as a defense mechanism that is keeping them trapped in their fear. Thus, they can begin to come from love, and know that they are always safe, that Life is always caring, compassionate, and for their highest good. Once this is realised, each role player can learn and understand:

AFFIRMATION:

The Oppressor learns when coming from love:
"I AM RESPONSIBLE FOR CHOOSING TO RESPOND LOVINGLY, RATHER THAN REACTING TO FEELINGS AND THOUGHTS THAT TELL ME OTHERS ARE WRONG, KNOWING ALL IS PERFECT IN MY WORLD".

The Rescuer learns when coming from love:
"I AM RESPONSIBLE ONLY FOR MYSELF AND ALLOW OTHERS TO LEARN FROM THEIR EXPERIENCES THAT I PERCEIVE TO BE WRONG, KNOWING ALL IS PERFECT IN MY WORLD".

The Victim learns when coming from love:
"I AM RESPONSIBLE FOR ALL THAT HAPPENS IN MY LIFE, AND I CHOOSE TO EMPOWER MYSELF, KNOWING ALL IS PERFECT IN MY WORLD".

The following two diagrams were invented by Margaret Mulqueen and myself. The first shows how each defense maintains and reinforces limiting behaviour, with fear being the controlling factor.

When we are living our lives in a state of unawareness, we tend to make judgements on people and situations. Following this we can choose one of three patterns of behaviour to act out.

1. Become the Oppressor, judge, criticise and attack a passive personality.

2. Become the Rescuer, judge, and justify our actions or the actions of others by defending our or another's victim position.

3. Become the Victim, judge that we are wrong, which can make us defend passively, or we can reach breaking point and eventually counter attack against an oppressor. Helplessness and indifference maintains the victim role.

THE DEFENSE TRIANGLE

UNAWARENESS
Judge

RESCUER
Justify

Fear

OPPRESSOR
Criticise

DEFEND ←→ Passive ←→ ATTACK
(Indifference)
VICTIM

The Freedom Triangle shows when we give up our defenses and come from love, perfection becomes a conscious experience. When we give up our self-defeating roles of Oppressor, Rescuer, and Victim through greater awareness, we also find we have let go of our defences that no longer serve us. Initially, this can make us feel vulnerable. As our self Trust and safety builds up as the result of practicing the Five Components, Breathing, being Aware, Accepting, Surrendering, and realising that all is Perfect, our aliveness increases, along with compassion and a Oneness with all Life.

THE FREEDOM TRIANGLE

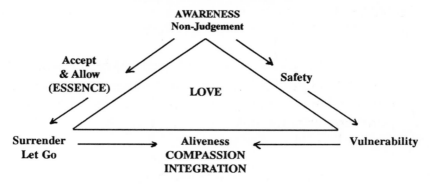

It is the defenses we build to protect ourselves that damage us, and not the outside threat which in reality is non-existant. It is only our inner belief in victimhood that maintains the outer threat.

Having described the three basic negative behaviours found in the Manipulating Triangle, let us consider living in harmony with others in our lives, without defenses. Living without defenses means coming from awareness and love, as well as being assertive without being aggressive. We know we are coming from love and speaking our truth when we express ourselves in the following ways:

LOVINGLY ASSERTIVE:
* Being able to express feelings, ideas and repeating them even under pressure.
* Total honesty and yet sensitive to other people's feelings.
* Saying what we mean directly without violating other's rights.
* Expressing our wants without putting others down.
* Expressing our truth without apologies or hostility.

* Having self confidence, respect for others and not needing approval.
* Letting others know where we stand, what we want, and where they stand with us.
* Being direct, unafraid of disapproval, yet sensitive to others.
* Not having to prove anything to anyone.
* Giving ourselves permission to live the way we want to, and allowing others the same right.
* Totally loving ourselves.

This list is endless, and it could be helpful to add ways you can Lovingly Assert yourself in the world:

*   _____

*   _____

*   _____

*   _____

CHAPTER THIRTEEN

BELIEF SYSTEMS

Awareness of how unhappy we are begins our liberation from it. Suppose we were told to give up the beliefs and values that suit our pleasures and desires; this would be good advice, but totally meaningless until we begin to suspect that our current beliefs might be the cause of all our problems. Yet, while unsuspecting, we continue to assume that our present beliefs are not limiting us in any way. And while hanging onto them, we falsely credit ourselves with being so intelligent and wise, and yet, we still have our anxieties, angers and fears. We can change nothing for ourselves until we 'wake up' to what we do against ourselves. Marcus Aurelius, the great Roman Emperor, once said,

'Those who do not observe the movements of their own minds must of necessity be unhappy'.

The beliefs I hold true to myself now are my limitations - true or false?

Everyone who has trained with me as a Breath Therapist, has been asked this question. All belief systems whether they be positive or negative, are the building blocks for 'life scripts' or personal laws, and consist of a set of opinions which most people are unwilling to give up. And who can blame them. Afterall, to give up such an ego is like giving up a part of ourselves

A person with a burning belief in, for example, a new found religion, will be highly motivated to spread the word and show others the power of faith which has enriched their life and given them purpose. This positive side of religion has done more for healing in the world than all the doctors and politicians put together. Indeed, faith is the cornerstone of most orthodox religions. On the negative side, a person driven to convert unbelievers, can fall victim to his own fanatasism and manipulate and force their faith on unwilling recipients. Some early missionaries destroyed complete cultures of civilisations in some countries, and the world is poorer because of it. *"A fanatic is one who can't change his mind and won't change the subject."* - Sir Winston Churchill. To kill in the name of God was once widely considered justification enough to convert the so-called heathen. The real reason was to protect man's burning passion to convert the world to his way of thinking. There is some evidence of this thinking even today.

Almost everything we have ever learned has come to us from outside ourselves, through our parents, books, teachers, religion, television, and observations of our environment. Most of these are based on other people's interpretations of what they perceive to be the truth. As we view the world through our conditioning, might it not be so that they are mere expressions of the ego? The only truth that can ever be real is the inward message coming from Higher Consciousness.

There was once a pilgrim, travelling through the desert, on his way to visit his holy shrine. He had travelled this way many times and knew the desert, and the location of each oasis on his way. One day he came across a weary traveller moving in the opposite direction, and obviously lost and out of water. He refilled this unfortunate soul's water bags and gave him directions to the next water hole. But, this man was adamant that no water hole could possibly exist where the pilgrim directed. He consulted his map and insisted there could not be one there, and that he must continue in his present direction. The pilgrim sadly shook his head, wished the weary traveller good luck and continued on his known path. He glanced back at the lonely and lost soul, who was ever intent upon following his map that was outdated and no longer useful. The pilgrim had met such travellers before and knew that no amount of explaining where the water holes were would ever convince them. He often wondered what drove people to destroy themselves in the effort to prove a particular point of view.

My own teacher, Michael, gave me a wonderful lesson on viewpoints when he once asked, "how many rooms are there here, where we are sitting?". The four of us students looked at each other, puzzled as to what the master was talking about. After we had each given what we thought to be the answer, and one of the more advanced students saying he thought there were five rooms, which totally perplexed me, Michael continued. "Very good, but there are six rooms here.... there is one for how each of us perceive it.... and then there is the real one. You must never forget that as you move your point of view, so will your universe change".

A buddhist monk in the Himalayas will view the world differently to a middle class American living in New York City. A communist perceives a different world to that of a capitalist. A Christian's view will be different to that of a Hindu even though at some high level, they are all saying the same thing, that human happiness is the goal. Each one's approach and view point will be quite different.

In the context of belief systems there are three levels of understanding.

1. SHALLOW BELIEF - Such a person holds a fairly shallow ideal that will change their belief with the first contrary idea that comes along. For example, if I tell you that the supermarket is down the street, around the corner and next on your left, you will probably believe me. You have no reason to doubt what I say. So, you follow my directions and on arrival, you discover the supermarket is not there. You no longer believe what I told you. Belief is easily changed at the first sign of evidence to the contrary.

2. BLIND FAITH - Nothing will change this person's mind, not even the threat of death. Their faith is so strong and often so blind because the person has shut themselves off from opposing or different ideas. Such people can be great achievers, but also fanatical defenders of 'the faith'. Their approach to life can be somewhat like the weary traveller, searching for the water hole in the desert. In spite of the pilgrim's invitation to change direction, he must stay with what he believes. Yet, the pilgrim feels no great need to try and convince the weary traveller of his folly. The pilgrim has been there and had his fill. He knows.

Any person who feels they 'must' convert others to their way of thinking, does so because there is a shadow of doubt in their own minds, which they of course would hotly deny. Their evangelistic assertiveness often comes from a sincere desire to change the world into a better place, but it is also often tinged with self-doubt and a need for self-verification. There is a need to have others support their belief as a kind of insurance that they are right after all.

3. SELF-UNDERSTANDING - A person with self understanding 'just knows'. Their knowledge comes from within. Nothing needs defending because such a person knows that the truth is strong enough to stand on its own. There is no driving need to win converts but a quiet relaxed sharing of knowledge that will allow others to reach their own inner knowing in their own time. Nothing else is necessary. This is Wisdom.

All the beliefs we have, may or may not be true. Real growth happens when we open up to the possibility that some of our beliefs and attitudes may not be true and therefore need re-examining.

Truth just is, whereas beliefs have our conditioning mixed up in them, and that is why we defend them so strongly. Like all beliefs, opinions and judgements, the application and use of them fixes them like concrete into our reality, thus we become controlled by them. It is important to understand that beneath everything we think, feel or do, is an attitude and a conviction. For example: Hear a person say - "I am annoyed that he should speak to me like that!" The anger probably hides an unconscious belief that really says "I am unworthy", and thus he or she attracts people to be unkind in order to verify the belief. Our current reality depends upon all our convictions being proved right, and this is a vital point. Can you imagine what would happen to our perception of reality if we woke up one morning with everyone in our life suddenly, for no apparent reason, refused to talk, love us, while resenting, and rejecting us. How would our self-image, our beliefs about us being the person we think we are handle the situation if our spouse, lover, children, boss, customers, and everyone else, suddenly began openly ignoring us. I suspect we would not cope at all. Our actions will always prove or verify our beliefs. The stronger the belief, the more a person's whole creative mind and body will work to create the exact reality that corresponds with the belief syastem. You see, our reality is based upon our beliefs, and this is good news when you consider that by changing our beliefs, we can change our reality.

Yehoshua (Jesus) preached faith and what he was saying is that faith is the most important step in the beginning. The journey begins with faith, but faith is not the aim. It is a means to an end. The aim is Self-Understanding, through the 'inner' experience of Higher Consciousness.

In one of Michael's lessons on the Qabalah, I remember him saying:

"Here is what so often happens. Some great teacher who has some real knowledge of Reality comes along, and is able, through story, fable, and above all, through the example of his/her life, to communicate some of that wonder, that mystery, and that 'inner' experience to their followers. Such is the power of the message and the teacher, that even after their death, the followers can pass on some of the experience, but not all of it, just as they did not get from the teacher - ALL his/her experience. Soon, after a generation or two, the experience begins to get 'watered' down and replaced with more and more of the teachings. In time, perhaps several thousand years later, all that is left are the stories, the fables, and the organisation which has grown naturally and inevitably to pass along the teacher's teaching and experience. But, by then, it is nearly all the 'teaching' and hardly any of the 'experience'.

When someone has the experience, even a little of it, they recognise the experience of reality in another and know that the thought, the words, the culture, the religion sounds and looks different, yet underlying them is the One Reality. But, if all you have is an explanation, a teaching about reality, then you must defend it against different explanations for it is all you have. This is the tragedy of time past. Let us speak clearly now, lest it all continue to be the tragedy of time future, (as it is of time present, often enough).

THE BEST EXPLAINERS OF REALITY ARE THE POETS, THE ARTISTS AND MUSICIANS. But far more important and useful than this dubious assertion, is this:

ALL THE TEACHINGS OF THE GREAT TEACHERS, ALL THE CREEDS AND RITUALS OF THE GREAT RELIGIONS, ALL THE STORIES OF THE GREAT MYSTICS ARE POETRY.

We must, we must, we MUST learn to treat them as poetic visions of how the One Unmanifest links with the One manifest. When you begin to treat them as logical, carefully reasoned metaphysical or philosphical or scientific discourses, then all is soon lost in a maze of nitpicked shit.

The last couple of words were not said merely to shock the fastidious, but were carefully chosen to convey a specific and important idea".

The idea is that just about everything that goes on in the conscious mind is the result of conditioning which is controlled by the ego.

Yehoshua gave us the message when he said "the kingdom of God is within you". He spoke of the Higher Self, which becomes realised as we become clearer. It is not beliefs we need.

The world is full of them.
It is more self awareness.

It is easy to get lost in all the different approaches to Spirituality. One person says this and another says that, and all claiming to speak the truth. Some even say that other religions are true, but ours is the total truth, or truer.

One weekend, I decided I would spend it visiting as many different churches and philosophical view points as I could. I first went and celebrated at the local Jewish Synagogue, then, I sat in on a discourse at a Hindu Ashram, followed by a Catholic Mass, then on to a Baptist, fundamentalist Church. I meditated and discussed philosophy with a group of Buddhists, I went chanting with the Hare Krishnas, and finished the day receiving Communion at the Church of England Cathedral. I was familar with all these groups prior to this venture, and I was struck all over again at the enthusiasm of their beliefs and conviction, that they carried the light of truth for all humanity. And in a way, that is true. Each approach was addressing to their followers the truth that was needed to be heard by that group, a truth that corresponded with the philosphical or Theological approach being talked about and with the individual that sat and listened. I returned home at the end of the day feeling inspired, uplifted and with a lot of gratitude. My faith in humanity reinforced and thankful for all the valuable work being done by all those church leaders. the differences in their beliefs no longer mattered. They were all saying essentially the same thing, and that 'Love' is at the centre. That is really all that matters!

GEMS ALONG THE WAY:

* The beliefs about myself, others, and my world may be my limitation.
* The need to defend a truth suggests there is doubt.
* Everyone views life in their own unique way, and that is Great!
* Self-Understanding that comes from the Inner Experience is a Truth worth listening to.

CHAPTER FOURTEEN

PERSONAL LAW

THE INDOCTRINATION PROCESS

Many limiting thoughts and beliefs are transmitted from generation to generation, from parents to their children in the form of an indoctrination process. Many parents don't consciously try to pass on their beliefs, but it happens at a subconscious level anyway. Children learn by seeing how their parents treat themselves. If a parent models self rejection and a lot of fear, the child will often imitate these traits. A new born child is very receptive and impressionable to the thoughts and feelings of all those around him or her, especially at birth. Signals of basic life attitudes are communicated by parents on a continuous non-verbal basis in the way they approach, touch, and express themselves to the new born. The parents every fear about life is picked up by the child.

As the child grows these messages are reinforced with verbal warnings such as "careful you will hurt yourself"...."lookout, that's hot"....."oh you are so clumsy" and so on. No doubt the parents protective stance is aimed at the child's safety and health, however it also effectively communicates the parent's basic life beliefs. Check out any playground and you can see anxious parents looking on, ever protective against their child falling off the swing, etc. The fears were already there in the parents, received by them at the time of their own births, and now passed on to the next generation.

As the parents integrate their fears through a process like 'Breath Integration', their projection process which could hinder the future growth, love and self expression of the child begins to change. The child begins to respect the fire, and not fear it. To respect their elders not fear them. To respect the traffic not fear it. To respect themselves and not fear any aspect of life. There is no formal training for parents, yet, the best preparation prospective parents can do for themselves is become more conscious. Conscious parenting is a process of clearing the old habitual belief patterns, and then making each step from conception, pregency, birth, and upbringing as conscious as one is able. Don't worry about developing the child's awareness, rather, work at developing one's own.

DEPENDENCY:

In order to be loved, the child adopts the beliefs and conditionings of the parent. If the child feels it is not receiving unconditional love from the beginning, he or she learns conditional love, i.e. the conditions under which the parents will give their affection and this is called approval. If the child did not perceive itself receiving enough unconditional love from the beginning, it will spend the rest of its life seeking love's substitute, approval from everyone he or she comes into contact with. The 'need' for approval makes a person vulnerable to being manipulated, and controlled by others in being made to feel guilty, anxious, or bad by the threat of disapproval. This can make them into an emotional cripple. The effort to get approval, if ignored by the parent, causes many children and adults to learn that the next best thing to getting attention is to get disapproval "love me or hate me but don't ignore me". Being "good" or "naughty " are two behaviour patterns which children learn to use to manipulate their parents into giving them the attention they crave for. This perpetuates the family conditioned belief structure which is based on fear and it becomes very entrenched. Even when the parents stop disapproving or die, the individual continues his or her thought patterns of self disapproval. The prisons are full of self re jecting people who use anti-social behaviour as a means of attracting dissapproval from a parental figure (the law).

Basic ideas about infancy are that we are dependent upon other people, and this gets misinterpreted that we are dependent upon other people for our survival forever. This gets carried over into adult life with beliefs that we can't make it on our own. As an adult, we know intellectually that we don't need others to survive, but if the subconscious belief operating is that we do need others for our survival, then we emotionally fall apart when people desert or leave us. Subconsciously, the message is that we will die, which would have happened as a baby, if others had not taken care of us.

THE TWO LAWS:

There are two types of laws operating in the universe. The first is Universal or natural law which is governed by the laws of physics and controls all existence. Depending upon how conscious we are depends upon the number of laws we are governed by. All laws are mechanical, that is, an outside agency is needed to create a response. Thus, the universe is controlled by the law of cause and effect. whereas consciousness is not mechanical, and therefore the more conscious a being is, the more it has the capacity to create it's own reality.

The second type of law, which is equally mechanical, but is man-made, and can be called 'PERSONAL LAW'. These are created by each indiviudual for themselves within their consciousness. Personal laws, because there are more than one ("My name is legion," he replied, "for there are many of us." Mark 5:9) are ideas and thoughts we have come to believe at a deep subconscious level. Once these ideas establish themselves into our belief system at such a deep level, they become the controlling factor of how we think and behave. Personal laws are beliefs that we no longer question, and regard as realities of truth, which reinforce the base level of consciousness upon which our life's script is formed. *"Convictions are more dangerous enemies of truth than lies."* - Friedrich Nietzsche.

Our life scripts or personal laws are created from conclusions we form from experiences. From experiences we form beliefs and from beliefs come the establishment of Personal Laws.

Once a personal law is established it can remain a conviction or a belief system for the rest of our lives even in the face of convincing and opposing ideas. We simply shut off from all ideas that threaten our personal law, which already believes it "knows" how it all is. Most of this is subconscious, for example, if a person has always reacted to criticism with anger, then every time they are criticised it is as if someone has pressed their anger button and they automatically becomes angry. He or she has little or no choice, it is automatic, a reflex action, and they become activated.

The subconscious is that part of the mind which stores our programmed and conditioned beliefs, which means most of our beliefs are unconscious. For example, if we conclude at the age of eight months that there was something wrong with us because we felt rejected by our mother while being weened, then that decision was recorded in our subconscious memory banks and filed away. For the rest of our lives and until we find a way to unlock that decision, the subconscious mind keeps replaying that conditioning every time it is activated by some event relating to our self worth which involves other people. When certain situations occur, such as the prospect of meeting a group of strangers, our old tape will be triggered and we will play what has previously been recorded. We will be stuck with replays of the past instead of responding to the reality of the present moment.

Once as a child we were made to share our toys with our cousins before we had finished playing with them ourselves. Our resistance to share was cut short with the toys being taken off us with a comment "don't be selfish, share your toys". The resentment we felt was mixed with feelings that we were in some way bad for being selfish. Later in life, this probably resulted in a deep feeling of "I don't deserve, I am selfish, I am bad".

If we believe at a core level that people hurt us, due to our being handled roughly at birth, then we will probably attract people into our lives who will satisfy this belief of a hostile environment. If our conviction is that life is a struggle then we will always do things in a difficult manner. If we are convinced that we are not good enough we will always perform in a way that will produce disapproval from others which reinforces the disapproval of ourselves. Also, we can push ourselves to 'try' harder even when we have approval, because we still believe we are not good enough, and do not believe others when they tell us we are doing well. If we always fail to achieve in most endeavours it is because we subconsciously believe we will eventually fail anyway. We can begin with the best intentions of success but subconsciously we sabotage our efforts and we will not even be aware of what we are doing. As a new born we only knew truth, we had not learned to lie as yet and had no ability to discriminate between what was true and what was false. We concluded that everything must be true, however our judgement was not alway correct and what we concluded then at birth can remain a personal reality for the rest of our lives.

HOW CREATING OUR OWN REALITY WORKS:

Thoughts are incredibly powerful. Everything that manifests itself in a person's life is a direct results of his thoughts - "as a man thinketh in his heart, so is he". We, as thinkers, are creative with our thoughts, and as creative beings we create with our thoughts. We in fact create our own experience. If we have the idea that we are limited in some way, then our mind will obey and prove that we are, by attracting events into our lives that will verify our beliefs. The mind is always right, because it is always manifesting its personal law.

Self Realisation is all about taking charge of our thoughts. As the ruler of our own thoughts, we then have the ability to create our circumstances. Thoughts have such a range of power that this makes us virtually unlimited, and the boundaries of what we can do extends to the scope of our thinking processes. The limitations of our thoughts are self imposed based upon our beliefs and then created by what we think.

The duality of good and bad, right and wrong, become non-issues once we realise that everyone is right in his or her mind. Someone reading this and thinking it is nonsense is right. To them it is nonsense and to argue with them is pointless. Most people believe that life is just something that happens to them, without any idea that they are creating it all, much like a self-fulfilling prophecy.

So these patterns may need to be identified and reversed. We can reverse them by learning new patterns of thought, and new ways of behaving. In other words, we create a new type of reality, a reality that supports our aliveness, joy and growth. This is best achieved by living the 5 Components and using them at every opportunity. This is helped by observing our personal self expression.

NEGATIVE LANGUAGING: - A REFLECTION OF OUR PERSONAL LAWS:

The use of words is a very strong indicator of personal laws operating within a person. Everything we say, every thought and feeling we have, every action we perform, is a form of affirming, of asserting our beliefs and declaring one's own truth as one sees it. Listen to the idle comments of people which reveal their beliefs. :- "You just can't win".."life is really hard" .. "the only way to get ahead in this world is to work hard".. or "with my luck it'll never work!". These are the beliefs which turn every event into proof of a personal philosphy of failure.

If we have been affirming a set of negative beliefs all our lives, we may need to balance up the scales with statements and affirmations of a positive nature. The most direct and easiest method of creating positive statements is to simply reverse our negative thinking. We may need to reconstruct our thoughts. For instance, everytime we catch ourselves making a negative statement, correct it by saying out loudly on the spot "I just said I couldn't do that, of course I can do it".

149

It must also be remembered that positive affirmations are really another form of conditioning. Most of us are conditioned into believing that positive conditioning is better than negative conditioning. In terms of personal experience in the world, this may be true. Yet, the aim is to be to be free of all conditioning, all belief systems that control how we think, feel and act. Yet, to get from negative conditioning to being free may be too large a step in consciousness for most us. So, positive statements can be used as a stepping stone to freedom.

Where we believe we are NEGATIVE, CONDITIONING	SELF ACCEPTANCE	Where we really are FREEDOM

In fact, we are free right now, as you read this. Yet, we are not free because we believe we are not. The only difference between a free man and one who is laden down with sorrow and fear, is his beliefs. All we have to do is give up our beliefs in bondage.

Types of personal Statements:
1. NEGATIVE, STATEMENT says - "I'm not good enough.
2. POSITIVE STATEMENT says - "I am good enough."

Because we have to say it suggests it may be untrue. They still work but the next step is easier.
3. SELF ACCEPTANCE says - "It's O.K. to be as I am".

I don't recommend using personal Statements that imply a need to change from a bad position to a good or even a better position. We need to accept where we are at, and to acknowledge our negative conditioning. It needs to be recognised for what it is before we are able to Integrate it.

For an effective use of affirmations refer to the book "Rebirthing Made Easy" or "Your Right to Riches".

It is important never to push negative thoughts out of the mind or struggle against them. What you resist, PERSISTS, and often reinforces our fears and negative beliefs. Even though we wish to be consciously free of our negativity, we are still committed to our unworkable beliefs at a subconscious level. Therefore, we need to change our basic beliefs which support the negative thoughts and conditionings in place. We start doing this when we cease using energy to support negativity, and begin focusing it on that which is true, even though we may still not fully believe in it.

Many people deny that they think negatively, yet they blame external forces for the negative events that happen to them. They have failed to realise the connection between their thoughts and beliefs and the things that happen to them.

If negative thoughts come up during the day, acknowledge, and accept them as a part of your purification or cleansing process. When a person begins this type of self Inner work, because of their heightened sensitivity and expanded awareness, it is easy to become triggered by associations of the past. During such times it's best to focus our full awareness on such feelings and where they are happening in our bodies. This begins to Integrate the pattern and the departure of another ego.

Such a departure often has a sense of loss with a greiving process accompanied with the Integration. It's like say goodbye to an old familar friend, as trouble some as he was. Attachment

151

to the ego knows no bounds. This acknowledgement of any activated material that comes up, is very important as long as we don't become identified with the thoughts and feelings.

I often say to my clients and students that the negativities we are aware of are no longer a problem. They no longer control us, even though they may feel uncomfortable, and their influence remains for a while. When we bring the negativity within us under the light of awareness, it dissolves. While we remain in a state of unawareness we remain trapped.

The struggle and conflict we see in our outer world is a reflection of the struggle and conflicts in our inner world. Our unconscious commitment to ideas of conflict that keeps us unconsciously angry will attract situations of conflict in our outer world. Clear our inner world of disharmony and watch how our outer world changes. What is happening in the conscious and subconscious minds, acts like a magnet and always attracts the circumstances it needs to verify its belief. That is why, all these well-intentioned people who rush around trying to bring peace to the world, in fact, achieve very little. They might do better for world peace if they spent some time looking at their own fear.

It is not surprising that most of us grew up with the idea that we were victims of other people and circumstances. The beliefs mostly formed at birth get reinforced with additional messages from people close to us as we grew up "No you mustn't - can't do that...You are too young... be careful, you will hurt yourself.. . don't touch you will break it.. you should be ashamed of yourself you bad child... children should be seen and not heard".

Basically our ego which is our personal law is concerned with survival and is often related to a perceived traumatic birth.

We have been struggling to survive ever since. Even our unconscious death urge is seeking an escape from a perceived hostile world. Our survival behaviour related to our birth however has been modified to our current experience. What we want is blocked off by what we fear, which is ultimately non-existance, death, in order to cover up our fear we play roles which are socially accepted, for example, miss nice girl and mr. good guy which is a cover up of a belief that we are in fact a bad person.

As a result of our early life conclusions from before birth until now, we started the suppressing process. This is the beginning of "the world is against me" syndrome which we have carried ever since. These impressions control us unconsiously and influence every area of our lives. Some of these conclusions could include:

Life is a struggle,
The world is hostile and against me,
People hurt me,
I am not wanted, there must be something wrong with me,
I can't get enough (air, love, money, time).
I'm not good enough / I am bad.
I don't deserve love.
Pain follows pleasure.(result of feeling pain at birth after the comfort of the womb).
I can't trust anyone.
Nobody understands me.
I can't get what I want.
Others are more important than me.

This list is endless, and each personal statement is an unconscious belief system that controls each individual in the type of life they lead, the people they mix with, the careers they choose, who they marry, their self esteem, and every other area of their lives.

Most people walking the planet right now are still carrying these types of personal laws which needs Intergrating.

The first step towards releasing these limiting beliefs is to get in touch with them. The Breath Integration process is probably one of the most effective means in achieving this. Another way is to look closely at our feelings, which can be traced back to a belief. In the next chapter, we discuss how to do this.

CHAPTER FIFTEEN

PERSONAL LAW CHART

As already discussed, our personal laws control our whole approach to life. They are so basic to our personality that they seem more like a fact of life than mere beliefs. A personal law is the ego through which we see and respond to every life experience. They are our Protective Barriers. The reason they are so difficult to locate and unravel is because we think we are our personal laws and to unravel them and let them go seems like losing a part of our true selves. The importance of becoming aware of the unconscious part of our false selves cannot be over emphasised if we are to become free of it and grow to Self Realisation.

The following chart is a quick and effective method of locating personal laws, that I have found useful in working with clients over the years. By getting in touch with the feelings, we can trace back to the original core belief that still controls us. Each column represents either an emotion, thought, behaviour or belief pattern that keeps us stuck in our misery. Following through each column brings us to the unconscious core belief that controls our whole perception and how we approach life. Even though this chart is a generalisation of how we process beliefs and personal laws, it is a very powerful and effective method for locating them.

155

The process works like this:

1. Become aware of the emotions - often the first indication of a personal law being activated.

2. Then become aware of the thoughts one is having which are supporting the emotion. These are the judgments and conclusions which begin to form beliefs (what am I telling myself?)

3. Then become aware of the behaviour and the 'self-sabotaging' games being played out to conform with our personal laws.

4. The first three columns are the defense mechanisms, and in observing them begins to reveal the personal laws in the fourth column - the false negative beliefs behind the behaviours, thoughts and emotions. This is the bottom line and the most important column to become aware of.

5. The fifth column gives us Affirmations to correct the imbalance.

Notice that the first three columns are our defense mechanisms, and the Personal Law is the protective barrier.

PERSONAL LAW CHART

EFFECT		EVENT	CAUSE	SOLUTION
EMOTION	THOUGHT BEHIND EMOTION (WHAT I'M TELLING MYSELF NEGATIVE STATEMENT)	BEHAVIOUR	(PERSONAL LAW) BELIEF BEHIND THOUGHT	POSITIVE STATEMENT
← DEFENSE MECHANISMS			←| ← PROTECTIVE BARRIERS →	→ FREEDOM
ANGER	Others are wrong Nobody understands me It's not fair It's your fault.	Lashing out. Losing Temper. Blaming.	World is against me.	Everyone is right. It's O.K. for things to be this way.
BOREDOM	I can't be bothered. No point.	Lethargy. Disinterest.	I'm not good enough.	I am interesting and can do anything.
CONTROLLED RESENTMENT	People have power over me.	Manipulated, put-down, controlled, passive.	I don't deserve to be alive.	I love myself & am in charge of my own life.
DESPAIR	I can't do it. I don't give a damn.	Indifference, Aloofness.	Nobody understands me or cares.	I love myself & others stand ready to serve me.
DISAPPOINT-MENT	It's not fair..	Unreal expectations of others.	I am powerless.	I am in charge of my own feelings.
DISTRUST	People are out to get me.	Getting ripped off.	Everyone is dishonest. Unsafe universe.	People always treat me fairly.

PERSONAL LAW CHART

	EFFECT	EVENT	CAUSE	SOLUTION
	EMOTION	BEHAVIOUR	(PERSONAL LAW) BELIEF BEHIND THOUGHT	POSITIVE STATEMENT
	THOUGHT BEHIND EMOTION (WHAT I'M TELLING MYSELF NEGATIVE STATEMENT)			
	— DEFENSE MECHANISMS ——→	←——— PROTECTIVE BARRIERS ——→		——→ FREEDOM
EMBARRASSMENT	I am ashamed. What will others think.	Withdrawal, Wanting to escape.	I'm not good enough.	I welcome this as a learning experience.
FAILURE	I never succeed. I'm stupid.	Failure, frightened to try anything.	I'm not good enough.	I am a winner. I always succeed.
FEAR	I'm in danger. I'm going to be punished/hurt.	Fight / Flight syndrome.	World is hostile. People and things are dangerous.	The universe is a loving & safe place.
FRUSTRATION	Life has to be perfect. I am powerless.	Intense drive to succeed, uncompromising.	I have to struggle to survive.	It is safe to stop struggling. Because I am love, I no longer need to demand it from others.
GRIEF	This is a loss forever. I have lost all that matters.	Withdrawal. A sense of loss.	I can't survive on my own.	Life is wonderful on my own.
GUILT	It's all my fault	Violent & Anti-social behaviour.	I'm a bad person.	I am a perfect child of the universe.

PERSONAL LAW CHART

——— DEFENSE MECHANISMS ———→ |←— PROTECTIVE BARRIERS —→ FREEDOM

EFFECT		EVENT	CAUSE	SOLUTION
EMOTION	THOUGHT BEHIND EMOTION (WHAT I'M TELLING MYSELF NEGATIVE STATEMENT)	BEHAVIOUR	(PERSONAL LAW) BELIEF BEHIND THOUGHT	POSITIVE STATEMENT
HOPELESS-NESS	Poor me.	Depression.	I'm unloveable.	I am loved & in charge of my life.
FEELING IGNORED	Nobody notices me.	Exhibitionist/Actor etc.	I'm bad. I don't deserve to exist.	Everyone notices me.
INADEQUACY	Nobody notices me.	Passive or chest thumping behaviour.	There is something wrong with me.	I am a beautiful Being.
INDECISION/ DOUBT	I may make a wrong decision.	Procrastination.	I am a mistake.	All decisions are right. It is safe to decide.
INSECURITY	I need approval/ security.	Perfectionist, nice guy/ girl act, manipulative.	I can,t get enough love/ money/air, or anything.	I have enough love and trust for myself.
JEALOUSY	Certain people & possessions belong to me.	Attachment/dependency	I'm not loved or good enough.	I am loved whether I'm with someone or not.

PERSONAL LAW CHART

—— DEFENSE MECHANISMS ——→ ←|— PROTECTIVE BARRIERS —→ FREEDOM

EFFECT		EVENT	CAUSE	SOLUTION
EMOTION	THOUGHT BEHIND EMOTION (WHAT I'M TELLING MYSELF NEGATIVE STATEMENT)	BEHAVIOUR	(PERSONAL LAW) BELIEF BEHIND THOUGHT	POSITIVE STATEMENT
JUDGING	They are bad. I must/should/ought syndrome.	Self righteous.	I will be punished if I'm bad. Pleasure leads to pain.	Everyone is doing the right thing at the right time in the right place.
LONELINESS	I'm always alone. I have nobody. Nobody wants me.	People drop out of my life.	It's unsafe to reach out. There is no one for me.	People love to be with me.
PHYSICAL PAIN	Sickness is a part of life.	Accident prone, often sick & in pain.	This is a hostile universe.	I am getting healthier every day.
REJECTION	I don't want to be here. I'm unwanted.	Strong leaving pattern. Leaving relationships / jobs, etc.	People always reject & leave me.	I am complete & total within myself. I am love.
WORRY	What if ...	Play safe, frightened of commitment.	People & things can hurt me.	Everything always turns out perfectly.
WORTHLESSNESS	Others are more important. I hate myself.	Self - put-down behaviour. Egotistical & conceited.	I don't deserve love. I am bad.	I love every aspect of myself.

There are numerous variations to the above, Yet, I have personally found these to be the main areas where Personal Laws operate.

During 1987, and my friends who were around me at the time will recall, I kept losing things, every day I couldn't find something and frustrated myself with endless searches for keys, appointment books, phone numbers and notes written months before that I wanted for this manuscript. Kathryn pointed out to me in one of our Breath sessions together that I was committed to a subconscious belief in loss. The universe, according to my Personal Law, was limited and that loss of important things was inevitable. She made me realise that the universe was infinitely large and what I could not presently find was still somewhere close by and would remain out of my reach until I had learned the lesson that nothing could ever be lost. There is change but no loss. We live in an abundant universe which supplies our every need if we let it. It was quite amazing, here I was telling people how to use affirmations without fully practising them myself. Everytime I lost something I would immediately say "I can't find it, I've looked everywhere, I just can't find it" and continue frustrating myself. What I was doing was reinforcing my belief in loss. I worked with these affirmations at Kathryn's suggestion;

"There is no loss in higher consciousness, therefore I cannot lose anything that is rightfully mine"

"Nothing is lost, there is no loss in the universe, only gain".

The very same day that Kathryn gave me these affirmations it was put to the test. I discovered that I had lost my keys and my first reaction was "I can't find them". I stopped mid sentence and said "Nothing is lost, they are here somewhere, I know it". Within ten seconds I had found them, and I have sinced cured my losing syndrome. This technique really works.

CHAPTER SIXTEEN

COMMITMENT
THE LAST GREAT FEAR.

Commitment is an interesting word and there is a lot of fear surrounding it. There are probably as many different interpretations of commitment as there are beliefs.

The true meaning of commitment can be summed up in a fable:

There was once a young man who went looking for the perfect Guru. After several months of searching through the holy mountains and meeting a number of what he regarded as imposter Guru's, he finally found a man who told him that in a cave around the next bend in the road, he would find the famous guru he had been searching for. He had heard many wonderous stories about this particular Guru, and was eager to meet him. He rushed on and sure enough, the cave was there. He went inside, and to his disappointment, he found a little old woman wrapped in a blanket. This was not what he expected after all the stories he had heard about this famous Guru. She did not fit his description of what a true Guru should be. However, he sat down and asked her, "What do I have to do to become enlightened?" She answered that he must do two things. First he must give up his search for a Guru, and secondly, he must stop trying to be a better person than he already is. He stared back at her in amazement and disbelief. He had heard some ridiculous things from some of the other so-called Gurus he had meet along the way, but this took the prize. "That doesn't sound right to me. You don't even look like a proper Guru. To be enlightened, I must have to do more than that?", he answered. She replied with a hint of a smile on her lips,

"Oh, OK. You're right then, you do have to do more than that!" The young man stood up, left disillusioned, and went on searching for a 'real' Guru.

A year later, another man arrived at this woman's cave, entered, and sat down. The woman had her back to him as she meditated, facing the wall. He was sure she was aware of his presence, but she continued to ignore him. Time passed, but the man was determined to wait for how ever long it took to be accepted by the Guru. After 40 days of neither of them moving, he was feeling as though he would die unless he soon received some food and drink, but he dare not interrupt the Guru's meditation, and so he patiently waited. Suddenly, the two silences met, and he felt a strange sensation throughout his body, and an urge to make some kind of a statement, or declaration. He slipped off his right hand glove and tossed it next to the Guru. He noticed that she slightly nodded in recognition, but continued to ignore him. He then pulled out a knife and cut off all his hair, and tossed it beside her. With that, she turned and faced her student.

These actions were symbolic. The glove which comes from the hand means that the giver of the glove is ready to dedicate him or herself to the learning, to the Guru, and eventually to him or herself. For the time they spend together, the student will obey, serve, and totally commit to the Guru. The shedding of the hair from the head in the presense of the Guru is symbolic of surrender, and non-attachment to the ego. He had proved he was ready!

True commitment means FAITH, TRUST, and COM-PASSION, and without living the meaning of any of these three words, commitment will never be complete, and the messages from Life (Guru) will not be understood.

The Dictionary tells us that committment means to pledge, promise, consign, obligation, liability, responsibility, bind, give over, guarantee, vow, decision, resolution, determination, stand.

It is no wonder that so many people 'freak-out' at the mere suggestion of committing to an ideal, or philosophy, and especially a long-term loving relationship. It is common for two people to live with each other for years in almost perfect harmony, and then they both decide to get married. What often happens, is that the relationship goes sour and breaks up within a short period of time. They both end up dazed and wondering what happened?

I have often asked my client's and students to intuitively write down the first thoughts that come into their minds when they hear any of the following words: RESPONSIBILITY; MARRIAGE; COMMITMENT; PROMISE; VOW:

You can do this yourself, by sitting initially with eyes closed. Then look at each word in turn and write down the very first thing that enters your mind.

Most people report feeling trapped, fear, and being controlled. So, what we are looking at is not so much the word commitment, but the definition each person has surrounding that word. It seems for most people that they have attached a conotation to that word which makes any form of 'true commitment' unworkable. This can be taken further to include our definition of the word 'Love', which has a very close connection.

Most of us while growing up, experienced times when we felt unloved, unsupported, dependant, abused, hurt, manipulated, and forced into a behaviour designed to get approval. This often gets confused with the times when we were really loved, and this gets mixed up together to form in our minds a definition of the word love. From this confusion a conclusion can be made at the subconscious level that approval or conditional love is genuine love. That we are only loved if and when we behave in a certain way. This gets further confused with our negative experiences of being manipulated, abused, and made to feel guilty when a parent tells us how much they have sacrificed for us. Very soon, we have an unconscious belief that tells us that love is kind, nurturing and beautiful, but it also means being dependant, hurt, and used. This becomes the hurt, confused, and frightened child within, and remains buried in the subconscious mind, while as adults we continue through life with a superficial understanding that love is all the wonderful things we think it is. This is fine until the hidden true definition of love gets activated when we are faced with someone who gives us unconditional love over a long period.

Until that happens, we may have love affairs which are enjoyable, but never really satisfy us or last. Then one day, Mr or Miss 'Right' comes along, and our feelings are quite different from those in any other relationship. Initially, we feel all this wonderful love coming from them. Never have we felt so loved and supported. This person really means it when they say that they love us. Sure, we have heard that line before, but this time, there is a depth we don't fully understand. Then, after a while, the hurt child who remembers our true definition of love, (the confusion of love being beautiful but also being painful, manipulating etc) gets activated, and we want to run and get away. Our lover, even though they are showing us unconditional love, a purity we have never really experienced before, starts to bring up all our fears around love and commitment. Sondra Ray once said that true love brings up everything other than itself. We want to be loved. It is what we have been searching for all our lives. Yet, when true love comes, it activates our subconscious definition of psuedo love that we concluded all those years ago as an infant. If we have a hidden definition of love that it is kind and it also being manipulating, hurtful etc, then that is what starts to come up in our consciousness, and we want to escape. All we can feel is that we are going to be trapped. Afterall, who really wants to be loved if it's going to be 'painful'? The sad thing about it is that this whole situation is unconscious, and that is why so many people block themselves off from having a truly successful, long-term relationship. If the relationship survives this setback and the two people get together, what gets triggered is that they fall into the same patterns and role playing within the relationship their role models (parents) played; Oppressor, Rescuer, Victim. Combined with the patterns copied from their parents, and their definition of love mixed with a poor self esteem, it is no wonder so many relationships end up being very unhappy, or not lasting for long.

When a person wants to back out of getting married at the last minute for no apparant reason, it is probably because their true definition of love and commitment has been activated. Such a belief pattern needs to be healed in order for each individual to find happiness and peace in their world.

When we look around us, we will see much evidence of unhappiness, and conflict in most peoples lives. Expand this and we will observe that this inner conflict gets projected out into International conflict, which is a spill-over of inner personal conflicts. Yet, on almost every street corner, every church, and in every family there is someone preaching the importance of love. Love is the answer they say. Compassion is the only hope for the survival of humankind. And of course they are right, but what is not understood, is that almost every person walking on the planet has a hidden definition of love that is quite opposite to what they would like it to be, or think it is. They are unconscious of their hidden fears revolving around love and commitment. They are simply quoting from some book or teacher, and lack the experience of true love themselves. Yet, everyone has the essense of love within them, which is like a crystal clear pool of water. But, when we concluded that love is also 'hurtful', it is like dropping mud into the pool. The love is still there as the water, and the mud makes the water (love) murky, and prevents us from seeing the bedrock bottom of the pool, which is Truth Itself.

There is not a more important subject in the entire world than healing within each individual, the hurt and confused child who has a false definition of commitment, marriage, and of course, love.

Margaret Mulqueen writes in her book 'Healing the Hurt Child Within'.

"The fear and/or experience of feeling trapped is very real for many adults. I believe this is a direct message to the adult from the child within who is saying loudly, 'let me out of here', or 'I have to get out of here'. Until we listen to the insistent cries of this child and are willing to free him/her from it's space inside of us, we will

continue to fear commitment, feel trapped and set up situations in our lives where because of the increasing pressure [from ourchild demanding attention] we have to get out of here, [leaving pattern]".

What is really being questioned, is not a commitment to something outside of oneself, but in reality, a commitment to oneself. With this understanding, true commitment reveals total freedom. Yes, there is complete freedom within commitment, because we are free within ourselves. That is the key. There is no freedom outwardly until there is freedom within. People demonstrate against oppressive governments, demanding more freedom, or complain about restrictive relationships, wishing they were free of it, never dreaming that they are their own prisoner. This is the tradegy of humankind, born from the fear and the unawareness of each individual. All the messages of love and goodwill, are but a drop in the ocean when they are expressed through the ego and unawareness. Yet, one small child, who has not learnt to unconsciously lie about love; one small child that expresses from its innocence is enough to save the world.

So, what is real commitment? How commited are we to face our fears, and become free of them? Do we respect ourselves enough to want the best life has to give? The steps to freedom begin and end with commitment. Commitment to oneself, to one's personal growth, and then to the world.

DETERMINATION:
Julius Ceaser landed in Britain with a small invading force. He knew his men were tired from the battles in Gaul and longed to return to Rome. Yet, he was determined to accomplish his task before returning home. He wondered how he could moti-

vate his small tired force against superior forces. He ordered his officers to burn all the ships. There must be no turning back. "We must go forward or die", he commanded his men. They went forward and won! We may question his motive to conqueur, and the worthiness of such an ideal, but we can admire his courage, determination, and belief in himself. These are the ingredients to success, and commitment.

Unless we are prepared to burn our bridges behind us, and move forward, we will remain stuck with our fears. You can't get to second base while keeping one foot on first.

But to be too frightened to try anything might be the easy way, but it lacks accomplishment, joy and ultimately, freedom. The person who has never made a mistake has never tried anything. Making mistakes is part of the journey, and a wonderful learning process.

Nothing can resist a will that is willing to stake its whole existence upon the accomplishment of a worthy ideal. This is true commitment. Such a commitment is enveloped with Faith, Trust, and Compassion.

FAITH is believing that truth will prevail and all that happens in the meantime is perfect and designed to enable us to arrive at the experience of 'knowing'. This gives us purpose.

TRUST is the courage and the determination to boldly step through the fear. This gives us direction.

COMPASSION is the power to heal the hurt child within. This gives us a sense of our Essence.

I have had clients in therapy sessions who spend a lot of time refusing to commit to their own healing and growth. Much of our work together was aimed at developing their personal commitment. Once they overcome their fear barrier, and 'went for it', they never looked back. At the beginning of the Breath Integration Process, some of these people using the techniques, and the strength of their commitment, eventually became excellent Breath Integration Practitioners themselves. And who best to help others, than those who have walked that way before.

CHAPTER SEVENTEEN

SIGN POSTS

There is a new breed of personal growth enthusiasts, who, in their search for truth, attend every seminar, read every book and listen to every inspirational cassette tape they can lay their hands on. After a period of time they have so much knowledge, but before they can put it into practice, they are off attending the next workshop that has come along. Such people could be called 'Seminar Junkies', and they are looking for that Master Guru, that special piece of knowledge, that height of 'enlightenment' that will give them eternal peace, love and joy.

The limitation could be that they are seeking truth outside themselves, and it will never be found there, for Truth is within.

This is not to say that books, seminars and tapes are a waste of time. I personally attend two or three seminars every year, and read widely, and gain much from them. Books, seminars, and teachers are sign posts to direct the way. They cannot provide the experience of the Ultimate Truth, which can only be an inner experience. I have known numerous people who have read all the books and have all the answers. In Spiritual terms they are not one inch further ahead than they were before they started, except having gained a lot of intellectual knowledge. I have known people to go to India in search of the living master who showed them the truth, and they have returned inspired, and uplifted. I have known others who did not go, but remained at home with family commitments, changing babies soiled nappies, dealing with family conflicts, and always aware of the passing drama in their lives. Their knowledge may not be as great, but their hearts are open with love and understanding. These are the true, unsung heroes, and their reward is that they experience the Inner Essense of themselves. The point is, Self Realisation happens right where you are in this present moment, and not on some holy mountain, or sacred shrine. If you go looking for it, you will never find it. If you open up your awareness, Self Realisation will find you!

A man went into a restaurant, sat down and asked to see the menu. He read it very carefully and with great enthusiasm. Having completed reading it, he suddenly began to eat the menu. On devouring it, he wiped his mouth with his napkin, stood up and left. On leaving, the startled waiter heard him mutter that it was very nice, but not much better than the last restaurant he had been to.

How many people live their lives like that in terms of their spiritual growth? How many get to only taste the menu and never get to experience the actual meal? How many become collectors of menus (techniques) and never do anything with them? Books and teachers provide the menu, the sign post, and it is up to us to do the inner work for ourselves which will give us that inner experience. Not to put into practice some of what is written here, or from some workshop you have attended is to experience little more than entertainment value.

If we went back to one of our first sunday school lessons that taught us "JESUS LOVES ME", and understood it, we would realise that the power of that message was telling us that we are loved unconditionally by Divine Love, because we are perfect. And that Divine Love will never be withdrawn even though some unconscious person may have told us we were 'sinners'. This may have caused us to lose our way if we believed them. Forgive, and thank them for giving us the opportunity to look further and begin to discover the Truth at last.

DIFFERENT PATHS.

It is wonderful that there are so many different techniques and systems aimed at Truth. Each religion, healing method and philosophical approach to wisdom has been formed because it serves people. Every guru and teacher has something to offer. The idea that one is better than another makes as much sense as saying that peas taste better than beans. The truth is that each person has a preference of taste and what serves one may not serve another quite as well. Comparison is only ego stuff anyway. After all, there is only one Truth and many paths to It.

When we presume that we have the only Truth for all humankind, we limit our creative expression and our compassion.

Many supporters of my work have called the five components as presented in Rebirthing Made Easy as the 'Sisson Method'. Some Rebirthers follow other Rebirthing methods such as 'the Groft' Method, Sondra Ray's L.R.T., Leonard Orr Method etc. Each have much to offer in their own right. I have closely studied many of these systems and support them. I put together the Five Components in this particular fashion because it served me the most and I guess many of my supporters found the same. The point I'm making is, it's not important which method you use, so long as it serves you the most and that we don't brand it as the best way for everyone.

By whatever method, I invite you dear reader, to consider most profoundly the importance of healing the hurt and frightened child within you. From Margaret Mulqueen's book,

'Healing the Hurt Child Within, she writes:

'The child within you, who has felt abandoned, unloved and ignored for so long, is waiting with an intense desire for your love and attention. When you are ready to open your heart and be lovingly present with your inner child, your adult self will experience healing and a deep sense of peace.'

You can heal this inner child by practicing the principles in this book and through the INNER ADVENTURE PROGRAMMES, which are designed to help you reach your own inner experience. Do this and you will be one more spark of truth, light and love, that will show the way for others to follow. Your guidance is so greatly needed. Your wisdom will be sought after. Your clarity, and your compassion will not only transform your world, but will inspire the rest of the world as well.

All that is written here is not new. We all have this knowledge already. Breath Integration, Rebirthing, Meditation, Yoga, and all the healing arts are not aimed at teaching you anything, but in unlearning all the untruths of fear and unhappiness, all the illusions, and letting go all that is not true.

Also, it is good to remember that the wonderful techniques and processes mentioned here are only a means to an end. They are not an end in themselves and it is easy to get stuck in making the process or the organisation that promotes it bigger than ourselves. Breath Integration is a wonderful process, but eventually we must go beyond techniques and drink from the ocean of Life and Truth. The process will help get us there more directly and then we can walk on - unaided and Self-Realised.

Much Blessings - COLIN P. SISSON.

APPENDIX 1.

ALKALOSIS:

Alkalosis is characterised by Hyperventilation and Teteny, (involuntary temporary paralysis of certain muscles of the body. Alkalosis is a physical condition which occurs when the P.H. (acid base) balance of the blood is altered from acid to alkali. This can be very significant for us as Breath Therapists and Rebirthers, as our client's are more likely to respond to Conscious Connected Breathing with tetany, and Hyperventilation, especially if their breathing mechanism is damaged as the result of birth trauma.

Tetany is common enough with new client's because of breathing difficulties, but this condition is aggravated by Alkalosis. It is often accompanied by a metalic taste in the mouth and hyperventilation.

Alkalosis is caused by taking 'Diuretics (except carbon anhydrase inhibitors). Diuretic medication (for those of us without a medical background), is taken for hypertension. It has the effect of removing excess fluid from the body, as well as lowering blood pressure and relieving congestive cardiac failure. This reduction of body fluid through the bladder causes a loss of potassium, leading to Alkalosis. The most common Diuretic medications are 'Thiazides' and 'Triamterene'.

Alkalosis can be brought on by the excessive ingestion of alkaline drugs, such as sodium bicarbonate for the treatment of gastritis or peptic ulcers. Also, through excessive vomiting causing a loss of hydro-chloric acid from the stomach. This loss leads to a reduction of 'Chloride Ions'. The condition of 'anerexia' can also be more likely to produce Alkalosis.

QUESTIONS TO ASK CLIENT'S BEFORE A BREATHING SESSION:

1. Are they on Diuretics medication? They will know if they are.
2. Have they recently had a 'stomach bug' or vomited? Give them a drink if they have.
3. Have they taken any alkaline medication such as eno, hardies, quickies, or anything with sodium bicarbonate or aluminium hydroxide in it?

For such client's, even more attention to keeping the exhale relaxed is important. Keep the whole breathing process more relaxed and not as deep. If they hyperventilate, get them to breathe into a paper bag or into their cupped hands. Above all, there is nothing to worry about with Alkalosis as it can be part of the healing process. But, this information is important to all professional Breath Therapists and Rebirthers.

INNER ADVENTURE PROGRAMMES.

BREATH INTEGRATION.
(REBIRTHING WITH THE FIVE COMPONENTS)

INNER ADVENTURE PROGRAMMES is an organisation to promote a series of training courses based upon the BREATH INTEGRATION PROCESS.

It is believed that the majority of people require a certain amount of guidance in finding their personal Teacher within themselves. There is an advantage to following pathways that have been carved into human consciousness by fellow travellers who have already found or are finding the storehouse of Wisdom within. It is also believed that the majority of seekers of truth, learn best in a clearly structured and well defined process of learning. For this reason, the following programme has been created by a number of dedicated people who are mastering their own Breath, who have studied the great Sages of history, and who are currently practicing their methods. These people have shown that they have the abilities to construct a programme of learning that is based upon the following:

*   It is Truthful.
*   It is Practical.
*   It is Experiential.
*   It is Dynamic.
*   It is Fun.
*   It is varied with Intellectual, Emotional, and Physical Processes.

INNER ADVENTURE PROGRAMMES:

TWO-DAY INNER ADVENTURE WORKSHOP:
This is an Introduction to Empowering ourselves and taking charge over our own lives, using the 'Breath Integration Process'.

NINE-DAY BREATH INTEGRATION (REBIRTHERS) PRACTITIONERS COURSE:
This is a course for those who have completed 10 Breath Integration, or Rebirthing sessions and want to greatly advance their growth, and learn to become a Practitioner.

NINE-DAY ADVANCE PRACTITIONERS TRAINING:
A course for Practitioners wanting to experience deeper levels of themselves, and learning important additional therapy skills.

NINE-DAY CERTIFICATED TRAINING COURSE:
The next step to greater learning and experience as an Effective Therapist, and discovering our Inner Divine Self.

TWELVE-DAY TEACHERS TRAINING COURSE:
By Invitation only, to train as a Teacher in presenting the Inner Adventure Programmes.
There are additional trainings available which include, PROSPERITY, LOVE RELATIONSHIPS, PERSONAL HEALING, THERAPUTIC BODY WORK, and others.

FOR FURTHER INFORMATION WRITE TO:
INNER ADVENTURE PROGRAMMES.
P.O.BOX 7264, Wellesley St,
Auckland 1, New Zealand.

GLOSSARY

Many of these following definitions may be different to those you would find in the dictionary. This Glossary defines words and phrases to explain exactly what the author means in the context being used.

DEFINITIONS

ACTIVATION: - Activation is a term that refers to becoming aware of suppressed energy patterns; the 'made wrongs' of the past. Activation can manifest as a negative thought, an uncomfortable emotion such as anger, sadness, jealousy, etc, or intense physical sensations in the body. Activation is being aware of any resistance in our being.

AFFIRMATION: - To affirm a statement of truth, or a belief.

ALKALOSIS: - This is a condition which occurs when the acid base P.H. balance of the blood is altered from acid to alkali, as the result of ingesting alkaline medications, or excessive and incorrect breathing. Refer to Appendix 1.

AUTHORITY DISAPPROVAL SYNDROME: - Negative beliefs and thoughts created as a result of our parents or other people in authority trying to control us with disapproval when we were a child and growing up.

AWARENESS: - Conscious perception of thoughts, emotions, or sensations in the mind or physical body. Awakening Awareness means being fully conscious of an energy pattern and is the second Component of Breath Integration. Complete Awareness means to experience our Divine Self.

BIRTH TRAUMA: - Birth Trauma is the result of mental impressions and conclusions we formed at birth about ourselves and the world we had just entered, which were mostly negative.

BREATH INTEGRATION: - Breath Integration is a technique using the Five Components, of which the breath starts a process to bring about Integration. The breath is used in the identical method as 'Conscious Connected Breathing', or perhaps better known as Rebirthing, with the additional four components to bring about Integration in a very relaxed, gentle and loving way.

COMPONENT OF BREATH INTEGRATION: - Any one of the five parts or techniques to bring about Integration during a breath session.

CONSCIOUS: - Perceived by the Self in the present moment. Awareness through observation of one's physical, mental and emotional environment.

CONSCIOUSNESS: - The Self being Aware.

DEATH URGE: - The unconscious desire to die or escape from a perceived hostile world, and negative experiences.

DUALITY: - Two separate and opposite principles - good and bad, positive and negative, night and day, yin and yang, female and male, etc.

EGO: - Ego represents all our conditioning, particularly the false limiting beliefs we have been taught, or adopted as being true.

ENERGY / A PATTERN OF: - Any thought, emotion or

physical sensation that one becomes aware of. Generally, a thought perceived kinesthetically, or a physical sensation.

HEALING: - Curing and releasing an illness at it's cause.

HYPERVENTILATION: - An abnormally high ratio of oxygen to carbon dioxide in the blood. The symptoms are experienced as dizziness, or breathlessness, and feelings of panic. It is caused by forcing the exhale and can happen during a breathing session to the degree that the breath is inhibited through suppressions and birth trauma. People who are afraid of their feelings can start to push on the exhale as energy patterns start to be activated. Relaxing more eliminates the symptoms, or breathing into a container like a paper bag or even your cupped hands, to balance the oxygen and carbon dioxide.

INTEGRATION: - Integration means to make Whole, and unifying the three functions, the intellect, the emotions and the physical. Integration is the goal of all healing.

JUDGEMENT / JUDGEMENTAL: - Discriminating between dualities of good and bad with a tendency to make people or situations wrong.

MAKE WRONG: - Comparing anything that exists in a negative context, to an imaginary standard.

MANIFESTATION: - To emerge into awareness or into existence.

NEGATIVE: - Anything that limits a person's aliveness, energy or compassion.

OTHER LIFE-TIMES: - Trauma that was created in a past-life

which has been brought into the present life to be healed.

PAIN: - A pattern of energy in the body that one is making wrong.

PERSONAL LAW: - A set of thoughts which has been conditioned into the subconscious mind to such an extent that it currently controls the belief system, which in turn control the behaviour of the whole person. Personal laws are generally unconscious.

POSITIVE: - Supporting one's happiness, power and compassion.

PROCESS: - A series or continuation of a method or technique to bring about positive change and Integration.

PROJECTION: - A perception that one's reality is congruent with one's model. A behaviour or belief one has that is mirrored back from other people, but one believes it to be not their own.

REALITY: - All that the mind perceives as being true.

REALITY/ULTIMATE: - All that is real, but not necessarily perceived as real.

REBIRTHING: - Rebirthing is a technique discovered by Leonard Orr in the early 1970's. There are many forms of Rebirthing used and each approach is aimed at Integration. The different methods range from a very cathartic approach to very gentle. Breath Integration uses the Rebirthing breathing technique as a basis and incoporates a number of additional techniques, altogether known as 'The Five Components'.

SELF-SABOTAGE CONDITIONING: - Any behaviour or

thought that is unconscious, that prevents us from experiencing joy, love, or achievement of some desired goal. There are twelve main ones: Self-Rejection; Limiting self labels preventing growth; Prejudice syndrome; Anger and resentment; Guilt and worry; Jealousy; Need for security; Hero worship; Procrastination; Right versus wrong categorising; Blaming and 'not fair' syndrome; Tyranny of musts, shoulds and oughts syndrome; and Fear.

SUPPRESSIONS: - The word suppression means to restrain, hold down, hide away and control. Suppressions are pockets of stress and tension which are created when there is conflict in the mind. Conflict is created in the mind when we try to avoid so-called traumatic experiences because we have perceived that experience to be bad, painful or unpleasant. In order to cope with major difficulties in our lives, our ego (learnt habitual conditioning) acts as a built-in safety mechanism and withdraws our awareness from the experience in order to cope and begin feeling better again, but in actual fact nothing can be avoided. When we try we only suppress that experience. That suppression acts as an energy block to our natural flow of love, joy and inner peace. It is here that all disease of the body begins.

TETANY: - Tetany is a physical condition of temporary involuntary paralysis of certain muscles as the result of Alkalosis. Once the Breath has been healed, tetany ceases to happen.

THE FIVE COMPONENTS OF BREATH INTEGRATION:
1. Consious Connected Breathing.
2. Total Awareness.
3. Total Acceptance.
4. Total Relaxation
5. Whatever happens is Perfect.

185

THE AUTHOR:

Colin P. Sisson was born in Levin, New Zealand on the 1st February, 1946. He was parted from his Father and two elder brothers, Robin and Warwick at the age of seven, when his parents separated. He lived with his Mother until he was fifteen, along with a caring Step-Father, Charlie, and a new sister Adrienne and brother Grant, children from the new marriage. Those eight years with his Mother taught him compassion and sensitivity, but he lacked confidence and a poor self esteem. When he was fifteen, he returned to live with his Father, who had since married Beatrice, a strong woman, and a stabling influence in Colin's life. His Father, a forceful man, gave Colin the lessons of determination, courage, self-motivation, and Integrity, important principles that have served him well.

With a Christian upbringing, his search for Truth and meaning in life really began as an infantry soldier on the battle-fields of South Vietnam during the 1968 Communist TET Offensive. Being a highly trained soldier, having trained with the New Zealand Special Air Service (S.A.S.), he served with distinction.

After returning from Vietnam mentally and emotionally exhausted, he took an interest in psychology in order to continue the search for himself, having glimpsed it on occasions through the terrors of modern warfare. His search led him to study Martial Arts, Buddhism, Hindu Philosophy, Christian Mysticism, the works of Gurdjieff and the Qabalah. Along the way he was introduced to many natural healing techniques like Massage, Rebirthing, Fasting, Counselling, Meditation, Yoga, Colour and Metaphysical healing.

A successful Counselling and Breath Therapist, Seminar Leader, and Trainer of many very successful Breath Therapists around the world. He has become successful at almost everything he has turned his mind to, and yet, he sees himself as no-one extra special. The early part of his life was chequered with disappointment and sadness. But having learnt his lessons well, he has become an inspiration to thousands who have participated in his Seminars and read his books.

Decorated for bravery with the 'Queen's Commendation for brave conduct', a civilian award. Author of the best sellers, 'Rebirthing Made Easy', and 'Your Right To Riches', and he is currently writing further works on healing and personal growth. It is refreshing to know a person like Colin, who has experienced the hard lessons in life and has been able to turn them into opportunities. His experience, intuition and compassion is a great inspiration to others as to what can be accomplished when we discover our own personal 'Inner Strength'.

KATHRYN RICHARDSON.

DISTRIBUTORS:

NEW ZEALAND   -   TOTAL PRESS Ltd.
                         P.O. BOX 7264
                         WELLESLEY ST.
                         AUCKLAND 1, N.Z.

AUSTRALIA   -   TOTAL PRESS
                         P.O. Box 758
                         SUBIACO W.A. 6008
                         AUSTRALIA.

U. S. A.   -   CONSCIOUSNESS VILLAGE,
                         CAMPBELL HOT SPRINGS
                         BOX 234, SIERRAVILLE
                         CA. 96126, U.S.A

EUROPE   -   AIRLIFT BOOK COMPANY
                         26 / 28 EDEN GROVE
                         LONDON N7 8EL
                         ENGLAND.

BIBLIOGRAPHY

REBIRTHING MADE EASY; By COLIN P. SISSON,
  Total Press Ltd. 1985.

YOUR RIGHT TO RICHES; By COLIN P. SISSON,
  Total Press Ltd. 1986.

HEALING THE HURT CHILD WITHIN; By MARGARET
  MULQUEEN, Total Press Ltd. 1990.

THE PROPHET; By KAHLIL GIBRAN, William Heinemann
  Ltd. 1980.

YOU CAN HEAL YOUR LIFE; By LOUISE L. HAY,
  Hay House.

HEAL YOUR BODY; By JAMES ALLEN, Hay House.

AS A MAN THINKETH; By JAMES ALLEN, DeVorss & Co.

LOVE YOUR DISEASE; By JOHN HARRISON,
  Angus & Robertson Pub. 1984

REBIRTHING ; The Science of Enjoying All of Your Life, By
  JIM LEONARD and PHIL LAUT, Trinity Publications

BORN TO WIN; By MURIEL JAMES and DOROTHY
  JONGEWARD, Addison-Wesley Pub.

THE COURSE IN SELF MASTERY; By PAMELA
  WHITNEY, Foundation of Peace.

I THINK, I BELIEVE, I KNOW; By CAROLE DAXTER.

CREATIVE VISUALISATION; By SHAKTI GAWAIN,
  Whatever Pub.

SECRETS OF THE INNER SELF; By DR. DAVID A.
  PHILLIPS, Aquarian Books.

THE BREAKTHRU GAME; By PACO, Total Press Ltd.
  1986.